AF127823

LET'S **REALLY** LEARN FROM PROJECTS

Bassam Hussein

LET'S **REALLY** LEARN FROM PROJECTS:

– A Study on Learning in Project Based Organizations

– The Ivar Aasen Project

FAGBOKFORLAGET

Copyright © 2020 by
Vigmostad & Bjørke AS
All Rights Reserved

First Edition / Printing 1

ISBN: 978-82-450-3412-7

Graphic production: John Grieg, Bergen
Cover design by Fagbokforlaget
Back side cover picture (Word Cloud) is generated in "NVivo"
and reproduced with the author's permission.

Enquiries about this text can be directed to:
Fagbokforlaget
Kanalveien 51
5068 Bergen
Tel.: 55 38 88 00
Fax: 55 38 88 01
email: fagbokforlaget@fagbokforlaget.no
www.fagbokforlaget.no

All rights reserved. No part of this publication may be reproduced, stored in a retrieval system, or transmitted, in any form or by any means, electronic, mechanical, photo-copying, recording, or otherwise, without the prior written permission of the publisher.

Dedication

Writing this book about the notion of learning and knowledge caused me to spend much time thinking about my mother and her journey in life. My mother did not have a fair opportunity to complete her aspired-to education, yet she remained a devoted and creative knowledge seeker. She combined that devotion with an immensely positive attitude towards the small and big challenges she had encountered during her journey in life. While writing this book, her journey has been a vital source of support and inspiration for me and therefore I dedicate the book to the memory of my mother, Diba (1942–2010).

Acknowledgments

I am so grateful to so many people. First and foremost, I wish to thank those who helped in the creation of this book, starting with *Bård Atle Hovd*, vice president of projects at Aker BP (formerly Det norske oljeselskap, also known in Norway as Det norske). Our collaboration between started in 2013, when I assisted Det norske in developing their tailored project management education programme for their staff working on the Ivar Aasen oilfield project. The collaboration with Det norske was extended in 2014 when we established an exchange programme between my department at NTNU and Det norske. Under that arrangement, senior project managers from Det norske visited NTNU to deliver lectures for students taking the applied project management course and in return I became involved in the company's efforts to develop a lessons-learned regime for the Ivar Aasen project. In the years 2016 and 2017 I was given a unique opportunity by Bård Atle to become even more involved when I was tasked with collecting and analysing the most important lessons learned from the project. During that period I also worked closely with *Torgeir Anda*, former communications director at Aker BP, who was a source of inspiration for me. Additionally, I thank *Bjørn Sundfær* and *Stine McIntosh* at Aker BP, with whom I have collaborated closely during the last six years.

Many people at Aker BP have openly shared their narratives and experiences from the Ivar Aasen project and in particular I thank the following: Monica Almvik, Øyvind Bratberg, James Carolan, Edvin Danielsen, Åge Ertsgård, Tonje Foss, Snorre Foussum, Hanne Gilje, Karl Johnny Hersvik, Geir Hjelmeland, Ivar Helge Hollen, Lars Petter Hoven, Michael Jensen, Tor Ole Jøssund, Einar Kvalø, Knut Jogeir Landa, Erling Rongland, Arne Sjursen, Stein Erlend Skei, Gaute Solberg, Inge Sunde, and Anita Utseth.

Additionally, I wish to acknowledge my former master's students from NTNU, *Asdis Sigurdardottir*, *Tryggvi Sveinsson*, *Kjersti Hoel*, and *Waqas Mushtaq*, all of whom conducted many interviews as part of their studies, during which they collected large amounts of data from Aker BP and the Ivar Aasen project. Their data subsequently proved of vital importance for me when writing this book.

Lasse Postmyr, editor at Fagbokforlaget, is much appreciated for his patience and valued support since the start of our collaboration in 2016.

Last, but not least. I thank *Stine*, *Marwan* and *Nora* who have been the source of comfort, love and joy that I needed in order to complete the writing of this book.

Bassam Hussein
Trondheim 4 April 2020

Prologue

Some years ago, I was asked to take responsibility for an educational programme in project management for a medium-sized Norwegian company. In preliminary discussions, the company's executives talked about the challenges they faced in their projects and how the intended programme should address those challenges. During the deliberations I recall that the director of the company said something like this:

> Our problem is not the mistakes we make during projects. Mistakes are useful because they help us to be aware of our shortcomings. The problem is the sense of the *déjà vu* we feel during each new project when we make more or less the same mistakes. It is frustrating to everyone.

The executives explained that at the end of each project the company was holding workshops and writing reports that covered the lessons learned, and that the reports were disseminated to everyone involved in new projects. Nevertheless, the same mistakes continued to be made on new projects and therefore the executives were seeking for advice on what they should do to avoid making same mistakes in the future. At the time, I did not have a very good answer, but my short answer was that they needed to focus on two issues. First, there was a need to work systematically in order to improve project management competency in the company, which was exactly what they were aiming for with the educational programme. Second, they needed to think about their method in order to learn from experiences and to ensure that they applied that knowledge to other projects and to the wider organization.

My response was a broad textbook answer to a difficult question and made me think about the topic of learning from projects and between projects, considering that failing to apply lessons from completed projects was not unique to the company. Such failure is rather the rule than the exception.

On another occasion, I served as a representative for the trade unions at NTNU on a large project for co-locating numerous departments following the university's merger with three university colleges in central Norway. The project included the construction of new facilities, as well as modification of existing facilities to accommodate the large number of students and employees who would be relocated to the newly merged departments. Possibly the most important *lesson learned* was that the project should not have been managed as mainly a construction and modification project, and that more focus should have been placed on creating environments for collaboration for faculty members, administrative staff and students in the newly merged departments. However, it took some time for upper management to realize the importance of changing their focus and project priorities.

After the completion of the merger project, the project groups were disbanded and members returned back to their daily work assignments. What happened to all the insights and reflections gained during the project? It is more than likely that in a similar co-location project in the future, similar misconceptions about the nature of the project will be made, and that the upper management will probably use valuable time to rediscover how such a project should *really* be managed. My own experience during the co-location project helped me to realize the importance of acknowledging the role of learning in managing projects. I realized that learning is not a mere outcome of projects. Rather, learning should occupy more dominant role during project development.

Discussions with many project practitioners suggest that learning during the course of a project is an attainable objective providing that the management encourage and support knowledge exploration and sharing. Most of us in the field of project management gain valuable experiences and utilize them in our next project. In this way, learning is to some extent preserved through the carriers of the knowledge (i.e. the individuals). However, the question about organizations' ability to take full advantage of individuals' learning and transfer it to their next project or to the wider organization is still a plausible ambition; currently, either it is not done or it is done poorly.

This book represents an exploration of the notion of learning in project-based organizations based on a combination of a literature study and extensive data gathered from a longitudinal case study. A bird's eye view of the existing body of knowledge on knowledge management and organizational learning literature suggests that the main reasons behind lack of improvements regarding project learning could be attributed to the failure to recognize the magnitude of efforts needed to learn in project-based organizations, particularly the following efforts:

- to enable individuals and teams in projects to learn from the tasks at hand through the process of experimentation, observation, reflection, conceptualization, and reuse of the existing knowledge in the organization (i.e. enable intra-project learning).
- to enable individuals and teams to share their own knowledge with other individuals or teams, or even the wider organization (i.e. enable inter-project learning).

Importantly, the two subprocesses of learning (inter- and intra-project learning) cannot be separated. Failure to learn anything of value within a project reduce the likelihood of producing any useful insights for future projects or for the organization at large, thus reducing inter-project learning capabilities in the organization. Conversely, adequate intra-project learning requires access to insights, knowledge and experiences gained from previous projects in order to create a fertile learning environment for individuals and teams in the focal project.

Many conditions need to be in place to facilitate or enable learning in projects or between projects. Such conditions are presented and covered in organizational learning and project management literature, and include management and individual commitment to learning, and not least cultural factors that encourage knowledge discovery and sharing. However, reports on the conditions are based on variety of approaches and perspectives on learning in organizations. Making sense of all previous research findings for this book has been a stimulating but challenging task. I have therefore sought to provide the readers with a thorough, yet condensed examination of previous research on project learning and present it in a structured and understandable format. Accordingly, I start with a review of various perspectives on and definitions of organizational learning. Thereafter, I present a closer examination of perspectives on learning in project-based organization. The examination includes making a distinction between inter-project based learning and intra-project learning, while also demonstrating their interdependence. Moreover, based on findings from the literature, I clarify and discuss the enablers and barriers to each type of learning.

My first lesson learned from conducting the research for this book is that enabling learning in project-based organization requires far more attention to *attitudes towards learning* than a focus on establishing procedures, systems or building knowledge repositories.

It is neither fruitful nor productive merely to affirm to individuals and teams that the management are committed to learning and knowledge. Insights gained from my research suggest that individuals and teams should experience that management actively translate their commitment into a multitude of efforts distributed over a long-term time horizon. Thus, the first focus of this book is to explore these efforts, both the means and the attitudes, that are needed to improve learning capabilities in project-based organizations.

I will show that learning and performance are not orthogonal dimensions that need to be balanced during project development. On the contrary, learning and performance are two mutually dependent parameters that have a circular relationship: various learning related activities contribute to improved performance and, in turn, improved performance contributes to greater appreciation of the role of learning in a project. In order for this circular relationship to thrive, a set of attitudes and enablers should be in place. Such enablers and attitudes are examined in this book.

The second lesson learned from my research is that most of the respondents and interviewees who contributed to the study strongly believed that learning is best achieved through direct interactions with colleagues, through other project team members within the focal project or within cross-projects and even outside the organization. In addition, they pointed to the difficulties associated with the search or capture of lessons learned. Findings from this study suggest that searching or documenting lessons-learned is a time-consuming process that occasionally conflicts with other project priorities.

Although the relevance and effectiveness of social interactions for enabling knowledge dissemination and acquisitions between individuals has been established, such interactions have limitations regarding the institutionalized level of learning (i.e. retention of knowledge for future projects) due to the temporality and cross-organizational nature of projects. Furthermore, findings reported in the literature suggest that relying on knowledge captured in repositories or in written reports is challenging for both contributors to knowledge and receivers of knowledge. The contributors of knowledge must be able to recognize the relevance of what they have learned outside their own project and then articulate and express that knowledge in comprehendible way, which might be a challenging task. By contrast, the receivers of knowledge must first comprehend and relate to the written knowledge before they can apply it in practice.

Thus, the second focus of this book is narrower than the first and focuses on improving the institutionalized level of learning in project-based organizations. Institutionalized learning refers to the footprints of learning from completed projects in the form *reusable* knowledge elements that could be applied to improve future projects or organizational capabilities. Therefore, in this book I present a process for performing post-project reviews. The main motivation behind developing this process was to enable lessons learned to be used in new projects. The entire process is described in detail, and findings are presented from several pilot tests that were carried out to learn more about the impact of the using the process.

For the above-described purposes, I draw on a case study of a mega project from the offshore sector – the Ivar Aasen project.

> The Ivar Aasen project is a NOK 28 billion oilfield development project that was successfully completed on December 2016. The project was executed under time pressure and a very tight market situation. Time constraints and shortage of suppliers and contractors proved challenging for both the operator and the project management team. The project consisted of several subprojects and was structurally complex, with over 120 suppliers and vendors, and in total more than 5000 people contributed to the project.

First and foremost, the Ivar Aasen project has provided some useful insights into learning in a complex and demanding environment that is characterized by continuous change, extreme time pressure, a multiplicity of stakeholders, tremendous financial impact, and market uncertainty. These characteristics render the project particularly interesting for study purposes and as a source of insights. Therefore, using insights gained from the Ivar Aasen project, this book addresses the following research objectives:

- Identification and elaboration of the means and attitudes needed to enable learning in complex and demanding project environment.
- Development of a process to capture lessons learned that enable an institutionalized level of learning and have value for future projects, for which the contingency thinking approach is used to identify the relevance of lessons learned to future projects.
- Identification of the lessons learned from Ivar Aasen, with the objective of gaining in-depth insights into the lessons learned from the project. In this regard the focus is on learning from both failure and success. These lessons learned could have value for readers who are interested in learning about and gaining insights into typical challenges, the means to respond to such challenges, and the drivers for success in a demanding and complex project environment.

Most importantly, the learning loop is closed and the following question answered: Did the case company learn the lessons from Ivar Aasen? If so, what has been the impact of on current projects? Answering these questions was done two years after project completion. Therefore, the case study is used to emphasize the significance of the long-term perspective with respect to learning from projects.

The Ivar Aasen project is a suitable case study because it was the first major project for Det norsk when it was a newly established company. The knowledge base for the company only existed in the heads of the individuals involved in the Ivar Aasen project. Therefore, opportunities for inter-project learning were limited. The operator company had to build not only an oil platform, with all its facilities and infrastructure, but also to build assets, a knowledge base, processes, an organizational culture, and systems to support knowledge acquisition and transfer. Thus, the project is a source of useful insights into the complexity of learning in cases when essential infrastructure for such learning are either not available or not adequate.

In addition, it is not an exaggeration to suggest that the survival of the operating company was dependent on the success of the project. Therefore, I believe that the project findings contribute to our understanding about the importance of learning in this context. The operating company was dependent on the project learning capabilities and the continued use of this learning to improve performance of the project towards success.

The Ivar Aasen project is used to understand the underlying factors that support learning in complex and demanding project conditions. In addition, the project provided insights into important reusable knowledge elements from complex offshore projects. This book contributes to the body of knowledge on offshore projects by presenting and discussing the significance of the aforementioned knowledge elements.

In addition, I believe that using a real-life longitudinal case study as a basis for this book could bridge the gap between practice and theory, and could offer readers the following advantages:

- The real-life example should help the reader to have a first-hand account of the significance of best practices and how they impact learning in practice. The reason is that just reviewing the literature is not enough to understand the best practices for learning in project-based organizations, given that organizational learning literature is largely abstract and conceptual.
- An opportunity to replicate or adapt the empirical inquiry to readers' own settings. This is based on my presumption that the ability to replicate will be further engendered by drawing on a real-life case.

Contents

Prologue 9
List of Figures 20
List of Tables 21

1 Introduction 23
1.1 Why is learning from projects challenging? 23
1.2 Why does learning matter? 24
1.3 Learning in project-based organizations 27

2 Organizational learning 31
2.1 Perspectives on organizational learning 32
2.2 The role of mental models 37
2.3 Transfer of learning 38
2.4 Contextual factors that support organizational learning 41
2.5 Impact of culture 41
2.6 Impact of leadership style and structure 43

3 Theoretical framework 45
3.1 Intra-project learning 48
3.2 Agile approaches to intra-project learning 52
      Adaptive life cycle models 54
3.3 Inter-project learning 55
      Cognitive view 56
      Social constructivist view 58
3.4 What is a lesson learned? 60
3.5 The role of post-project reviews 61
3.6 Novel approaches to support knowledge sharing 63

4 Study contributions 65
4.1 Research stages and research questions 66
4.2 The Ivar Aasen project 70
4.3 Contracts 72
4.4 Evaluation of the project 74

5 Enablers of learning 77
5.1 Introduction 77
5.2 Method 79
5.3 Findings: enablers 79
5.4 Findings: barriers 83
5.5 Discussion 85
5.6 Learning and continuous improvement in performance 86

6 Process for identifying lessons learned from the Ivar Aasen project 91
6.1 Introduction 91
6.2 The process 92
6.3 Participant selection 93
6.4 Data collection 94
6.5 Data analysis 96
6.6 Characteristics of the Ivar Aasen project 97
6.7 Learning from failure 100
      External challenges 102
      Internal challenges 102
6.8 The root causes of challenges encountered 104
      Front-End Engineering Design (FEED) of the topside 104
      Relationship with contractors and subcontractors 105
      Inadequate information flow between subprojects 106
6.9 Discussion of the lessons learned from challenges encountered 108
      Better FEED 108
      Need for better interface management between subprojects 109
      Need for building a 'one team' from the first day 110
      Need to focus on suppliers' dedication 111
      Need for transparency 113

6.10 Learning from success 113
    A good working environment based on trust and backing 114
    Quick mobilization 114
    Clear priorities 115
    The determination to succeed 116
    Autonomy 116
    Visible and supportive project leadership 117
    Dedicated project owner 117
    Turning points 118

7 Contingent classification of the lessons learned 121
    Organizationally complex project 122
    The Ivar Aasen project had significant commercial impact 123
    The Ivar Aasen project was carried out under time pressure and market uncertainty 124

8 Did we really learn the lessons? 127
8.1 Evaluation of the relevance and usefulness of the lessons learned 128
8.2 Evaluation of the impact of lessons learned 129
8.3 Evaluation of the reuse of lessons learned 134
8.4 Final remarks 138

9 Epilogue 141
9.1 Enabling learning in project-based organizations 141
9.2 Improving systematic capture of lessons learned 143
9.3 Capturing reusable lessons learned 144
9.4 Did we *really* learn? 144
9.5 Suggestions for future research 145

10 References 147

11 Appendixes 163
11.1 Appendix 1: Questionnaire – Subprojects 163
11.2 Appendix 2. Questionnaire – Supporting functions 166
11.3 Appendix 3. Questionnaire – Project management 167
11.4 Appendix 4. Questionnaire – Suppliers 169

List of Figures

Figure 1	Learning and performance in projects (Arthur et al. 2001)	26
Figure 2	Single-loop and double-loop learning (Argyris and Schön 1996, p. 22)	36
Figure 3	The four subprocesses of organizational learning (Crossan et al. 1999)	39
Figure 4	Learning typologies, outcomes and economic benefits (Prencipe and Tell 2001, p. 1378)	40
Figure 5	Framework of the study: Inter and Intra-project learning	48
Figure 6	Experiential learning (Kolb 1984, p. 21)	49
Figure 7	Intra-project learning summarized	51
Figure 8	Inter-project learning	55
Figure 9	Knowledge transformation, cognitive view	56
Figure 10	The SECI model (Nonaka and Takeuchi 1995)	57
Figure 11	Contribution of the petroleum sector in Norway (Norwegianpetroleum 2020)	65
Figure 12	Research stages	68
Figure 13	Circular relationship between learning and performance	89

List of Tables

Table 1	Various definitions of organizational learning	35
Table 2	Examples of definitions of organizational culture	42
Table 3	Summary: significant events in the project	72
Table 4	Factors that supported learning within the Ivar Aasen project	79
Table 5	Barriers to learning	83
Table 6	Selection of participants for interviews	94
Table 7	Summary of the main challenges	101
Table 8	Interface management problems between the subprojects	110
Table 9	Respondents' evaluation of relevance and usefulness of the lessons learned from the Ivar Aasen project	129
Table 10	Postulates to assess the impact of learning	131
Table 11	The impact of the lessons learned	132
Table 12	Ranking of the impact of the lessons learned	133
Table 13	Applicable and followed-through lessons learned from the Ivar Aasen project	136
Table 14	Applicable but not followed through lessons learned from the Ivar Aasen project	138

1 Introduction

Repeated errors are characteristic of organizational life (Busby 1999a). Duffield and Whitty (2015) maintain that many project-based organizations struggle with learning from projects and still fail to learn from their past project experiences.

A study conducted by Swan, Scarbrough and Newall (2010) indicated that even within highly project-oriented organizations much of what is learnt in a project goes no further than the project itself, or at best is transferred either through individuals who move on to new projects or through personal networks. Only occasionally does learning from projects lead to more institutionalized levels of learning.

1.1 Why is learning from projects challenging?

Projects are temporary systems that comprise a mix of different specialist competences that have to be applied in order achieve a certain goal or to carry out a specific task within the limits set for costs and time (Sydow et al. 2004). This view is informative of the transient and multidisciplinary nature of projects – features that fundamentally contribute to shaping the possibilities for, as well as the obstacles to generating knowledge and accumulating learning. Several scholars have attributed the challenges of learning from projects to the inherent features of project assignments, such as uniqueness and temporality (e.g. Prencipe and Tell 2001, Bakker et al. 2011). Due to the temporary nature of projects (Turner 2009, Kerzner 2013), there is a risk of individual experiences being lost when the project is completed. For example, the practice of having temporary positions, such as consultants, could lead to loss of knowledge when the holders of those positions complete their tasks and leave the organization (Schindler and Eppler 2003, Lindner and Wald 2011). Moreover, new encounters between people take place whenever a new project is started, which may increase the barriers to learning from the previous experience gained by others.

In addition, projects require cross-functional or cross-organizational resources, which make it difficult to execute the projects within the traditional organizational boundaries, which in turn complicates the transfer and reuse of useful lessons (Bresnen 2006). Furthermore, some projects may lack opportunities for regular contact with colleagues outside the project (Scarbrough et al. 2004) and that may reduce opportunities for exchanges of experiences and knowledge (Grabher 2002).

The uniqueness of projects is a factor that could inhibit learning. During project development, various forms of mishaps, errors and either unfortunate or good decisions might occur because of a particular combination people and problems or opportunities that might not occur again. Therefore, there is a popular claim that learning from history or past projects does not apply because circumstances change (Kransdorff 1996). This claim may lead to ambivalence regarding the role of project learning.

Additionally, the customized nature of some projects can reduce both the repeatability of projects and the potential for learning between projects, as particular situations, challenges or problems may never exist again (Brady et al. 2002). In turn, this may lead either to ambivalence regarding the role of project learning or that project teams may not be able to recognize its relevance outside their own project. Even if projects make their knowledge available, other organizations' units or teams may lack the absorptive capacity to recognize the value of new knowledge, as well as how to assimilate it and apply it to commercial ends (Cohen and Levinthal 1990, Bakker et al. 2011).

1.2 Why does learning matter?

Although the amount of new knowledge needed to deliver a project depends on the novelty and uniqueness of the product being created, projects still share many similar processes (Love et al. 2005). Valuable knowledge about good practices and methods for identifying the causes of errors and correcting errors is shared through the proses of identifying and sharing lessons, both within the project team and with other project teams, which either could help other project teams to avoid repeating the same mistakes (Brady and Davies 2004) or could help to refine existing ways of doing things while avoiding the risks of experimentation (Shaw 2017).

Learning is beneficial during the execution of the project because it can contribute to improved performance. For example, the results of a correlation analysis based on data from Australian construction organizations show that when the project reviews were carried out regularly, their project schedule growth was significantly reduced (Love et al. 2003). Although limited to construction firms, the study by Love et al. (2003) is significant because their findings correlate with the benefits of learning and performance.

Furthermore, learning is not only beneficial for ongoing projects but also for future projects (Kotnour 2000, Williams 2008). Learning is beneficial for future projects because during the project life, enormous efforts have to be made by the team members to solve problems or to respond to challenges (Damm and Schindler 2002) and the experiences gained could provide valuable insights for future projects (March 1991, Arthur et al. 2001, Bartsch et al. 2013, Ekrot et al. 2016). Failure to learn from such experiences may cause new projects to go through their own cycle of exploration in order to solve old problems, rather than exploiting knowledge that is already available in the organization. The expression 'reinventing the wheel' applies to such tactics in cases when existing knowledge and experiences cannot be accessed and used because they have not been stored and disseminated (Disterer 2002). Although learning from past experience is considered important for the success of future projects, some scholars question its potentials. For instance, March et al. (1991) points out that while learning from past experiences is important, they question the possibility when experiences from the past are limited or detached from context.

Also, learning is important for organizational success (Cooke-Davies 2002). Damm and Schindler (2002) denote this type of learning as learning about projects. Projects not only lead to recommended improvement measures for future projects but also leave footprints that are relevant for the wider organization. Such footprints may include learning about market situations, competitors, suppliers, technology application, partners, and customer bases. Moreover, learning from one project could contribute to improvements in existing project management processes within the organization (van Donk and Riezebos 2005). Therefore, Arthur et al. (2001) have argued for including learning as a success criterion in projects in addition to the traditional iron-triangle criteria, in order to make a full assessment of the project performance.

As shown in Figure 1, Arthur et al. (2001) suggest that a project that does not contribute to learning but manages to deliver according to expected performance criteria should be considered a false success, whereas a project that fails to deliver within the expected performance and yet manages to contribute to learning could be considered a hidden success. This is an interesting perspective and one that has not yet been adopted widely in project management practices. For this reason, Zollo and Winter (2002) have called for wider recognition of the role of learning in projects and they point out that other considerations, such as cost considerations, have a somewhat paradoxical effect of tending to suppress learning when it is most valuable and needed.

Figure 1 Learning and performance in projects (Arthur et al. 2001)

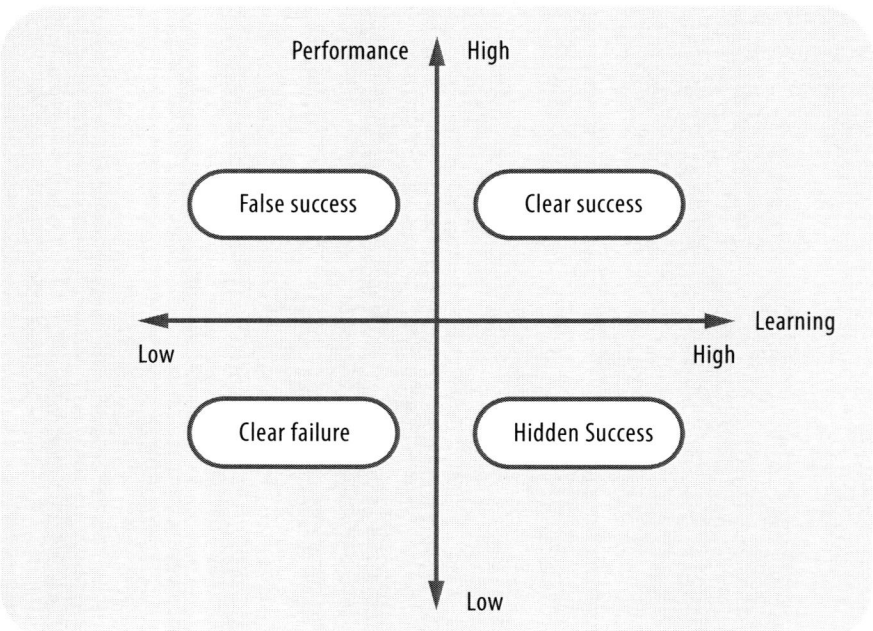

Despite repeated calls for the inclusion of learning as a success measure, it is still not clear which indicators should be used to measure learning success. Project learning impacts the individual level and can be assessed by assessing individuals' competencies before and after the project (Hussein et al. 2019).

By contrast, I argue that on the team level or project level, learning is observable through three clusters:

- The project's ability to make use of individual's learning in order to fulfil or to surpass the predefined performance goals of the focal project. Learning from this cluster is only observable through its impact on performance of the focal project.
- Improving performance of future projects. The project leaves 'footprints' in the form reusable knowledge elements or insights that could be applied to improve future projects or organizational capabilities.
- The impact on the learning culture of the individual, project and organizational level.

1.3 Learning in project-based organizations

Whereas in a functionally based organizations departments act as knowledge silos that preserve learning, project-based organizations lack the natural mechanisms for the knowledge acquired in one project to be transferred and reused by other projects. Therefore, the accumulated knowledge might be lost when the project group is disbanded. Progress in improving project learning appears to have been slight (Hartmann and Dorée 2015), despite the many efforts made to determine why organizations do not learn within projects or cross projects (Swan et al. 2010), or to identify the barriers to and enablers for learning from or between projects (Shokri-Ghasabeh and Chileshe 2014), or to understand the effectiveness of project reviews or other mechanisms for knowledge capture and sharing (Busby 1999a, Newell et al. 2006, Anbari et al. 2008, Rose et al. 2020).

The theoretical foundations of this book are based on the body of knowledge that focuses on and discusses learning in project-based organizations. Project-based organizations can be described as those in which most or all of the business activities are performed through projects (Hobday 2000) or that are entirely dedicated to one or more projects (Blindenbach-Driessen and van den Ende 2006). This is a common type of organization in diverse businesses, including engineering, construction, oil and gas, shipbuilding, and pharmaceutical businesses. Sydow et al. (2004) argue that the temporality of projects makes project-based organizations more suited to organizational change and innovation, as projects do not constitute irreversible resource commitments in terms of fixed costs. Sydow et al. (2004) further distinguish between two categories of project-based organizations. The first category is project-based organizations that are more customer oriented, primarily operate with short-term projects that are specific to identified customer needs, and share some distinct knowledge and learning characteristics:

- Typically, projects follow the stage-gate project execution model with predefined deliverables, performance goals and specifications. Thus, the teams involved in the project have to come up with more or less customized solutions within a strictly limited period of time. These project settings present unique possibilities to learn more about the promotion of knowledge development processes (Gersick 1988). However, the downside of being focused is that individuals care less or not at all about matters outside the project; having to work fast means that individuals have little time to reflect on and document experiences or lessons learned.
- Projects requires some degree of autonomy in order to allow project members to find the best possible way to produce the intended deliverables within the predefined constraints. The relative absence of hierarchy and the diversity of skills involved should provide fertile grounds for creativity and innovation (DeFillippi 2001, Swan et al. 2002). However, on the downside, being autonomous means that individuals or teams may develop a knowledge silo that is not available to members of other projects or the wider organization, thus reducing possibilities of inter-project learning.
- Projects require multidisciplinary teams. The teams and individuals come to the project with different knowledge bases and the diverse knowledge bases could accelerate innovation and problem solving. However, the downside is that individuals bring their own perceptions on how to interpret former experiences. In such contexts, project teams may have difficulty in developing into a unified group operating on the basis of shared knowledge (Wenger 1998). Enabling knowledge integration in such contexts is dependent on how well the individuals manage to connect their individual knowledge bases.

The second category of project-based organizations comprises projects with longer durations that are typically within the military and pharmaceutical industries. In turn that should give rise to knowledge and/or learning features that are not very different from those of permanent organizations.

In the next chapter I begin by introducing the concept of organizational learning as an umbrella concept for learning in project-based organizations. The aim of the introduction is to present the various perspectives on organizational learning. In addition, I explore the conceptual foundations of how learning is transferred between individual, group and organizational level, and finally summarize the factors that influence (support or hinder) the transfer of learning between those levels.

2 Organizational learning

There are many perspectives on organizational learning. However, common to all perspectives is that we cannot call anything learning unless the acquired knowledge is not exploited for something useful, such as the following: to improve performance, avoid earlier mistakes, leverage future projects, gain better insights into individual or organizational strengths or weaknesses, improve organizational performance, question rules and belief systems, develop new concepts to adjust behaviour to match rules and norms, or radically change the fundamental norms that govern the organization strategies. The complexity of learning in organizations in general is rooted in the fact that learning is a multilevel phenomenon involving individual, group, organizational, and at times population levels of analysis (Schwab 2007).

There is a general consensus in the organizational learning literature that organizational learning begins at the individual level and propagates through groups and up to the organizational level. For example, Simon (1996, p. 176) state: 'An organization learns in two ways: (a) by the learning of its members, or (b) by ingesting new members who have knowledge the organization didn't previously have.' Duhon and Elias (2008) claim that an organization knows something if just one person knows it, and it is the organizational culture and structure that enables knowledge to be reused effectively.

The move from the individual learning level to the organizational learning level is not simple. Ideally, for an organization to learn, individuals must first acquire knowledge (Huber 1991, Argyris and Schön 1997). Furthermore, Sydow et al. (2004) suggest that individual learning may simultaneously be a matter of organizational learning, when project members typically move from project to project. Similarly, firms may encourage informal spontaneous processes of knowledge exchange and not make any a priori attempt to transform individual learning into organizational learning. However, there is broad acceptance that knowledge gained at the individual level does not become organizational learning until its shared, integrated and institutionalized (Crossan et al. 1999). Therefore, it is important that organizations develop an awareness of the factors that influence the transfer of learning in order to build an effective learning capacity. In the following, I start first by revisiting the various perspectives on organizational learning. Then, I will explore the conceptual foundations of how learning is transferred between individual, group and organizational levels, and finally summarize the factors that influence (support or hinders) the transfer of learning between those levels.

2.1 Perspectives on organizational learning

Organizational learning theory was developed to lay the ground rules for achieving effective transformation in organizations through learning collectively in contrast to just individual learning (Dixon 2017). Although interest in the issue of learning in organizations dates back to the late 1950s, it grew almost unnoticed until a sudden explosion in the late 1980s (Easterby-Smith et al. 2000).

Despite a lack of a consensus on a definition of organizational learning, there is has been accordance on three broad perspectives that form the foundations of the definition (Sense 2007). The three perspectives are as follows.

Cognitive. From this perspective, learning is described as a system of information acquisitions, storage, retrieval, and transfer, regardless of whether knowledge is converted into actions (Tsang 1997). Learning from the cognitive perspective is attained by gaining insights into, and identifying associations between, past actions, the effectiveness of those actions, and future actions. Lessons learned from this perspective are mainly shared understandings of the organizational problems and possible remedies, and they constitute the knowledge base of the organization or corporate memory (Easterby-Smith and Lyles 2011).

Behavioural. This action-oriented perspective focuses on changing behaviours as a result of learning (Fiol and Lyles 1985). Tsang (1997) suggests that lessons learned from this perspective relate to changes that must be implemented to change the behaviour of individuals or organization in future, thereby institutionalizing the lessons learned.

Social constructivist. There are two schools of constructivism (Prince and Felder 2006). In cognitive constructivism, an individual's reactions to experiences lead to (or fail to lead to) learning. In social constructivism, meaning is not simply constructed, it is co-constructed. The social constructivist perspective challenges the traditional idea that learning takes place within the heads of individuals through information processing. It starts from the assumption that individuals learn by constructing knowledge through practice, and that learning is situated and occurs mainly through conversations between people within their sociocultural settings (Easterby-Smith et al. 2000). The social constructivist perspective suggests that learners are social beings who construct their understanding and learn from social interaction (Edmondson and Moingeon 1999). This view introduces stronger emphasis on socially oriented approaches to the understanding of learning and knowing.

Each of the above three perspectives on organizational learning is important for understanding how learning takes place within projects and between projects, as well as to understand how learning impacts the organizational rules, systems and structure. For example, the action-oriented perspective on organizational learning is useful for understanding how accumulated knowledge contributes to the implementation of changes at the project level or organizational level, such as through changes in procedures and process (Garvin 1993). The cognitive perspective is useful in order to understand knowledge as utility and how receivers of knowledge interpret, process, and frame and reframe the knowledge utility in their own contexts in order to update or modify their mental models (Huber 1991). The social constructivist perspective is useful to understand how learning within projects or between projects is linked to social interaction (Sense 2011).

Furthermore, it is necessary to clarify the difference between the learning organization and organizational learning. Although the two concepts are used synonymously, they do not have the same meaning (Örtenblad 2001), although to some extent the meanings are related (Tsang 1997). From a behavioural perspective, organizational learning is a process that unfolds overtime (Chiva and Alegre 2005), and focuses on integrating and institutionalizing individual learning, and converting it into actions for the organization's benefit (Garvin 1993).

By contrast, the learning organization resembles a *capability* of the organization that strengthens or enables individual learning (Phillips 2003). Garvin (1993) defines a learning organization as an organization that is skilled at creating, acquiring and transferring knowledge, and modifying its behaviour to reflect knowledge and new insights. A key feature of learning organizations is that they provide individuals with possibilities to learn from both their own experiences and from others' experiences, as well as to acquire and transfer new knowledge, and modify their behaviour according to newly acquired knowledge and insights (Senge 1990).

The main criticism of the organization learning literature is that it is largely too abstract and conceptual, and does not provide any concrete guidelines on how to achieve or measure the degree of learning achieved in organizations (Armstrong 2000, Caldwell 2012). In addition, many views on organizational learning complicate understandings of the concept. Tsang (1997) even argues that the number of definitions of organizational learning is equivalent to the number of writers on the subject. Fiol and Lyles (1985) attribute the confusion about organizational learning to the original definition provided by Simon (1969), who defined organizational learning as the growing insights and successful restructurings of organizational problems by individuals reflected in the structural elements and outcomes of the organization itself.

According to Simon's definition, learning within organizations consists of (1) the development of insights (i.e. a change to state of knowledge that is not clearly observable) and (2) the development of structural and action outcomes (i.e. changes that are more visible) (Simon 1969). Often, the two types of development do not occur simultaneously, which makes it difficult to distinguish them. As a result of such confusion, scholars with differing perspectives have understood organizational learning as new knowledge, new structures, new systems, or merely actions or some combinations of actions (for a summary of the definitions of organizational learning, see Table 1.

The perspectives listed in Table 1 may suggest that organizational learning relies heavily on knowledge sharing between individuals. The cognitive view of learning suggests that the knowledge of individuals is shared through information processing systems, while the social constructivist view suggests that sharing is best attained through social interactions between individuals.

Organizational learning from the behavioural perspective is linked to taking either incremental actions or radical actions in order to improve performance. Hence, Mayo and Lank (1994) suggest that it is not possible to draw any conclusions about organizational learning if we only reflect on experiences (i.e. about gaining knowledge) or state the lessons learned (i.e. by articulating and codifying knowledge) without taking any further action. Thus, either taking actions or adapting constitute an essential component in the behavioural

Table 1 Various definitions of organizational learning

Author/perspective	Contribution
Huber (1991) (cognitive)	The author looks at organizational learning from a cognitive perspective and suggests that learning does not necessarily need to result in changes or adaptations to behaviour. An entity learns if, through its processing of information, the range of its potential behaviours is changed. Alternatively, an organization learns if any of its units acquires knowledge that it recognizes as potentially useful to the organization. In this view, organizational learning is dependent on four subprocesses: knowledge acquisition, knowledge distribution, information interpretation, and organizational memory.
Stata (1989) (behavioural and cognitive)	The author reflects on the similarities and differences between individual learning and organizational learning, as both contribute to changing or modifying behaviour and actions. Organizations can learn only as fast as the slowest link learns. Change is blocked unless all of the major decision-makers share beliefs and are committed to take the actions necessary for change. Furthermore, learning builds on past knowledge and experience (i.e. on memory). Organizational memory depends on the institutional mechanisms (e.g. policies, strategies and explicit models) used to retain knowledge. In this view, organizational learning occurs through shared insights, knowledge and mental models.
Argyris (1977) (behavioural)	The author introduces the concept of single-loop and double-loop learning as responses to errors. Error refers to the discrepancy between what an organization planned to do and what actually happened when the plan was implemented. Single-loop learning does not question the rules but rather follows the rules when errors are detected. Double-loop learning is about questioning the rules and establishing new rules when errors are detected.
Fiol and Lyles (1985) (cognitive)	The authors clarify the distinction between organizational learning and organizational adaptation, and they show that change does not necessarily imply learning. There are different levels of learning, each of which have a different impact on the strategic management of the firm. According to this view, organizational learning is the development of insights, knowledge and associations between past actions, the effectiveness of those actions, and future actions. By contrast, adaptation means the ability to make incremental adjustments as a result of environmental changes, goal structure changes, or other changes.

perspective of organizational learning. This is further affirmed by Revans (2017), who maintains that 'there is no learning without action and no responsible action without learning'. The significance of taking actions as an important component of learning is demonstrated by Argyris (1977) in his contribution to the literature on organizational learning. As shown in Figure 2, Argyris and Schön's model can be compared with thermostat, as decisions are based on loop learning, whereby two loops are used to distinguish between two types of actions following the acquisition of knowledge in organizations:

- Actions based on single-loop learning (learning at individual or group level)
- Actions based on double-loop learning (learning at organizational level).

Figure 2 Single-loop and double-loop learning (Argyris and Schön 1996, p. 22)

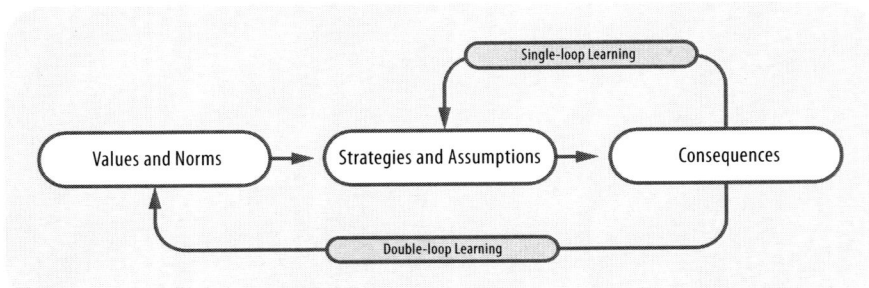

In single-loop learning, individuals or groups assume that the rules are correct and when mistakes and deviations are made, individuals then adapt their behaviour to mitigate the situation without revisiting the rules or the norms of the underlying structure. Fillion et al. (2015) refer to this approach as adaptive learning whereby, when observing from a single perspective, individuals adapt to the work to be performed. In single-loop learning the actions are taken to keep the performance within organizational norms and values (Schön and Argyris 1996). The major problem with single-loop learning is that it results in eliminating symptoms without focusing on the sources of the problems. A further problem with single-loop learning is that it assumes that the rules are valid in terms of time and context, which generally is not the case.

Double-loop learning occurs when an error is detected and corrected in ways that involve the modification of an organization's underlying norms, policies and objectives. In double-loop learning, the underlying causes behind the errors are corrected or changed by adapting or altering the rules, polices, norms, structure, and methods of working. Fillion et al. (2015) refer to this type of learning as generative learning.

2.2 The role of mental models

As indicated in the preceding subchapter, there is broad acceptance in the organizational learning literature that initial learning in any organization takes place at the individual level. The relationship between individual learning and organizational learning remains one of the contested issues in organizational learning debates (Antonacopoulou 2006). In order to understand the dynamics of learning in organizations, Kim (1993) suggests that we need to understand the interplay between learning and memory in individuals.

At the individual level, learning has two meanings: (1) the acquisition of skills or know-how (also known as operational learning), which implies the ability to operate or produce some action, and (2) the acquisition of know-why (also known as the conceptual learning), which implies the ability to articulate a conceptual understanding of an experience. While learning has more to do with the acquisition of knowledge or skills, memory has more to do with retention of acquired knowledge or skills (Lieberman 2012). Learning and memory are closely interconnected because what we already have in our memory functions as a framework for what we learn, and in turn what we have newly learned affects our memory (Lieberman 2012). In this context, memory is not only a static structure (e.g. a memorized multiplication table), but also includes active structures that affect our thinking process and the actions. Kim (1993) suggests that a good way to understand these active structures and how they are influenced by and influence learning is through the concept of mental models. Senge (1990, p. 8) describes mental models as follows:

> Mental models are deeply held internal images of how the world works, images that limit us to familiar ways of thinking and acting. Very often, we are not consciously aware of our mental models or the effects they have on our behaviour.

Therefore, individual learning can be described as a cycle of conceptual and operational learning that both informs and is informed by mental models (Kim 1993), and sharing these mental models is the only mechanism that allows for the transfer of learning between individuals, groups and the organization.

According to Senge (1990) and Kim (1993), organizational learning is created once individual mental models have become sufficiently shared throughout the organization. Schön and Argyris (1996) assert that people's actions are guided by mental models and that few people are aware of the models they use.

Rabkin (1995) argues that people will first try to notice the new, relevant variables and then integrate them into new mental models that can help guide behaviour. Ellis and Davidi (2005) affirm that the chances of integrating new variables will be greatly increased if people *intentionally* invest time and effort in the process. Ellis (2012) argues further that, if mental models guide people's behaviour or responses to various stimuli,

> Learning may be defined as the process of formulating and updating mental models. (Ellis 2012, p. 218)

2.3 Transfer of learning

Crossan et al. (1999) summarize useful insights into the processes that occur at the individual, group and organizational levels that enable the transfer of learning through feedforward and feedback loops. Feedforward loops allow learning to flow from the individual to the group and to the organization. Therefore, feedforward loops support *knowledge exploration* and expand the knowledge base for the organization. By contrast, feedback loops exploit what has already been learned in the organization to the group and individual levels, and supports *knowledge exploitation* and institutionalizes the learning results (Crossan et al. 1999), as shown in Figure 3. Crossan et al.'s four subprocesses are:

- Intuiting – seeing patterns and possibilities at the individual level.
- Interpreting (individual reflections) – explaining insights to others through narratives, images and words. This results in the establishment of a new view of the world or updating an individual's existing view of the world (individual's mental model).
- Integrating – developing a shared mental model and taking coordinated action through mutual adjustment of individuals' mental models. Thus, integration is about collectively deciding what is working and not working in the execution of a task.
- Institutionalizing – embedding the learning of individuals and groups into the organization through its systems, structures, procedures, and strategies for collective benefits.

Figure 3 The four subprocesses of organizational learning (Crossan et al. 1999)

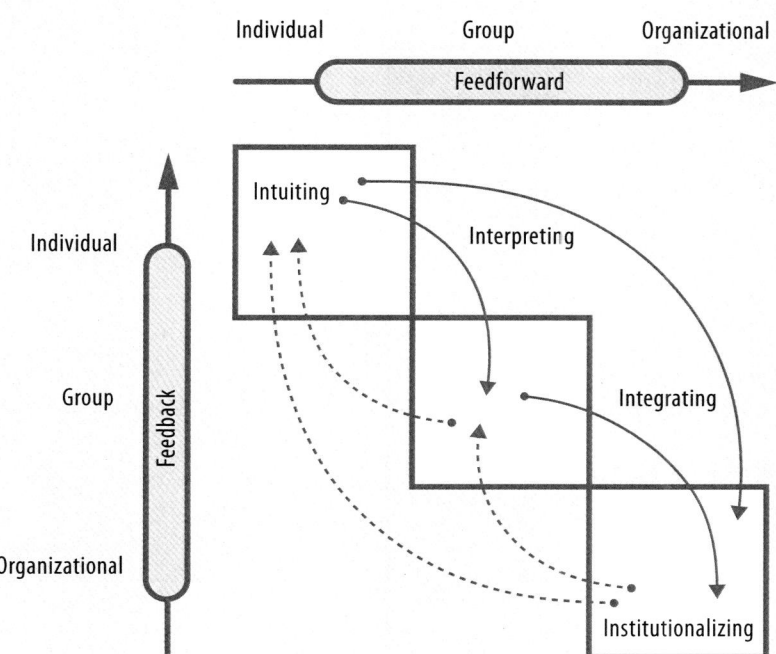

Swan et al. (2010) argue that although the framework developed by Crossan et al. (1999) can be used to explain the process of transferring learning between the various levels, it does not cover in detail the mechanisms that link insights formed at group level to organization level. Zollo and Winter (2002) have attempted to fill in this gap by distinguishing between three mechanisms that are needed to transfer learning between groups and to organizational learning:

- Experience accumulation: this refers to the tacit accumulation of experience by individuals over time and the use of that experience to improve practice in an incremental fashion.
- Knowledge articulation: this is a deliberate process through which individuals and groups determine what works and what does not work in the execution of an organizational task. Thus, knowledge articulation occurs when groups are engaged in collective reflection in order to gain insights (Edmondson 2003).

It follows that knowledge articulation combines the interpreting and integrating subprocesses in Crossan et al.'s model (Crossan et al. 1999).
- Knowledge codification: allows for knowledge to be accessed and used by others sometime in the future and is not dependent on personal networking.

Prencipe and Tell (2001) build on the model developed by Zollo and Winter (2002) and distinguish between learning typologies, outcomes and benefits within each mechanism. The learning landscape model developed by Prencipe and Tell (2001) is useful because it provides insights into the learning processes within each mechanism in project contexts. The learning processes, learning outcomes and benefits within each mechanism in Zollo and Winter's model are shown in Figure 4.

Figure 4 Learning typologies, outcomes and economic benefits (Prencipe and Tell 2001, p. 1378)

	Learning processes		
	Experience accumulation	Knowledge articulation	Knowledge codification
Learning typologies	• Learning by doing • Learning by using	• Learning by reflecting • Learning by thinking • Learning by discussing • Learning by confronting	• Learning by writing and rewriting • Learning by implementing • Learning by replicating • Learning by adapting
Outcomes	• Local experts and experiential knowledge in individuals (e.g. subject matter expert)	• Symbolic representations and communication • Improved understanding of action–performance relation (predictive knowledge)	• Codified manuals, procedures (e.g. project management process)
Economic benefits	• Economics of specialization	• Economics of co-ordination	• Economics of information (diffusion, replication and reuse of information)

2.4 Contextual factors that support organizational learning

There are several contextual factors in support of the feedforward and feedback loops to achieve learning (Wiewiora et al. 2019). However, there is no agreement in literature as to what these factors are or what mechanisms support feedforward and feedback loops. Commonly reported factors include organizational culture, structure and leadership style. These factors can be compared with the four contextual factors discussed by Fiol and Lyles (1985) and affect the probability that learning will occur: a *culture* that promotes learning; a *strategy* that allows flexibility; an organizational *structure* that allows both innovativeness and flow of new insights; and a stable internal and external *environment*. These factors have a circular relationship with learning in that they create and reinforce learning and are created by learning.

2.5 Impact of culture

Research on organizational culture began in the early 1930s (Park et al. 2004). Much of the research evolved from the construct of organizational climate into the field of organizational culture. Culture consists of the shared beliefs, ideologies and norms that influence organizational action-taking, and is seen as a facilitating factor or even a vital condition for both organizational learning and knowledge management to take place (Fiol and Lyles 1985, Marsick and Watkins 2003, Park et al. 2004, Rai 2011, Jasimuddin and Zhang 2014).

Furthermore, de Vries and Miller (1984) suggest that organizational culture can be used to predict the actions taken by an organization. Various definitions of organizational culture have been proposed in the organizational and project management literature, some examples of which are listed in Table 2. Nevertheless, general consensus on a definition organizational culture has not been achieved because researchers use diverse theoretical approaches and assumptions, and they interpret similar cultural phenomena in different ways (Belassi et al. 2007).

Table 2 Examples of definitions of organizational culture

Author	Definition of organizational culture
(Schein 1990)	A pattern of *basic assumptions* that are invented, discovered or developed by a given group as it learns to cope with problems of external adaptation and internal integration, and that have worked well enough to be considered valid and therefore to be taught to new members as the correct way to perceive, think and feel in relation to those problems.
Hofstede (1991)	The collective programming of the mind that distinguishes the members of one organization from the members of other organizations.
Alvesson (2002)	An umbrella concept for a way of thinking that takes a serious interest in cultural and symbolic phenomena. It includes values and assumptions about social reality, but these are less central and less useful than meanings and symbolism in cultural analysis.
(Blake 1969)	Routinized ways of doing things that people accept and live by Organizations have norms and values that influence how members conduct themselves, and these norms may prevent members from applying maximum effort or, conversely, may encourage them to do so.
(Yazici 2009)	The set of values, beliefs and behavioural norms that guide members of the organization on how to get work done.

Alvesson (2002) argues that many researchers who have studied organizational culture have generalized the concept when they are only referring to particular aspects, such as shared values. This is evident in the way that most of the organizational literature has classified organizational culture. For example, Cooke and Szumal (1993) classify organizational culture based on promoted norms and expectations, whereas Goffee and Jones (1998) based it on solidarity and sociability. Moreover, in the project management literature, similar classifications have been used in an attempt to establish the impact of organizational culture on project performance.

In discussions on organizational culture, reference is often made to the shared espoused and practised norms in the organization. Ajmal et al. (2009) suggest that an organizational culture with norms oriented towards learning will have a positive impact on learning culture at the individual, group and organizational level. Learning culture can be described as an organizational culture that is oriented towards the promotion and facilitation of workers' learning in order to contribute to organizational development and performance (Rebelo and Gomes 2011, p. 174).

Organizational culture influences the way individuals learn by influencing their behaviours (Zheng et al. 2010). In order to achieve a culture that promotes learning, different conditions have to be in place in the organization, such as both management's and individual's commitment to learning. In addition to these conditions Ahmed et al. (1999) and McGill and Slocum (1993) add that transparency, tolerance for errors, and trust are important conditions for achieving a learning culture.

Transparency is more likely to be a common practice in an organization where the degree of interpersonal trust is high (Wiewiora et al. 2014). Trust can be defined as the '*belief that relinquishing some degree of control over a situation will not lead to personal loss or harm*' (Moingeon and Edmondson 1998, p. 248). Extant research shows also that trust has a positive impact on knowledge-sharing activities (Al-Alawi et al. 2007, Lucas and Kline 2008, Mueller 2014, Wiewiora et al. 2014). According to Al-Alawi et al. (2007) the main reason for mistrust is superficial relationships between people. Therefore, the provision of possibilities to socialize and interact may contribute to greater degrees of interpersonal trust and therefore to improved knowledge sharing. Considering that trust and control coevolve (Inkpen and Currall 2004), the challenge is to find the right mixture of both (Atkinson et al. 2006).

In addition to interpersonal trust and psychological safety (Edmondson 2004), individuals must be willing to challenge the status quo and realize that innovation is a part of their job (Berwick 1996). There must be tolerance of errors to ensure that people will try new ways of doing things that might improve current processes without the risk of being punished if a mistake is made (McGill and Slocum 1993, Schein 2010). Learning requires people to share success and failure stories. Fear of consequences of disclosing failure or success leads to a culture that prevents feedforward learning.

2.6 Impact of leadership style and structure

Leaders are individuals who hold high levels of power to facilitate or inhibit learning in the feedforward and feedback directions (Vera and Crossan 2004). Hannah and Lester (2009) describe specific actions that leaders take to influence learning by promoting openness to diverse opinions and thereby facilitate transference of an individual's learning to a group. Actions include introducing policies and procedures that help to foster learning through knowledge creation and diffusion, such as through the introduction of reward systems, as they recognize and reinforce learning (GAO 2002). Internal competition between divisions in an organization can be a preventive factor in knowledge sharing. Hence, management's role is to prevent the situation and to promote knowledge sharing between projects (Hannah and Lester 2009).

Leaders who choose to tighten control at the expense of learning create a climate that prevents individuals from experimenting and sharing ideas with others (Edmondson 2003). However, it is important for leaders of the organization to encourage other members of the same organization to ask for help in order to improve learning (Edmondson 2004).

Fiol and Lyles (1985) suggest that organizational structure plays an important role in triggering learning processes. For example, matrix structures are associated with higher learning performance, whereas group autonomy (project structure) enables the exploration of new ideas and solutions. Autonomy protects the group from becoming overly exposed to existing organizational routines and norms (Benner and Tushman 2003). This in turn encourages exploration of a more diverse range of solutions and new alternatives. Argote et al. (2003) indicate that the ideal structure for learning is one that is loosely coupled and provides some degree of group autonomy while ensuring weak connections between groups and the organization.

3 Theoretical framework

The point of departure in this book is that in the absence of adequate and continuous means and attitudes for learning within projects and between projects, organizations repeat old practices, make the same mistakes, and improvements remain superficial and either incidental or short-lived. However, if relevant means and attitudes for learning are in place, one or both of the following advantages may be gained (Brady and Davies 2004):

- Learning could contribute to improved performance of the focal project and contribute to career development of the individuals, thus increasing the competence base in the organization. The competence base could contribute to better performance in the organization's other ongoing projects or in its future projects.
- Valuable knowledge can be reused in similar projects in the future or in ongoing projects, thus avoiding 'reinventing the wheel' or frustrating déjà vu experiences. Valuable lessons could generate a new knowledge base for the organization regarding projects that could lead to new business opportunities or to improve organizations capabilities.

Dixon (2017) affirms that the absence of learning in any organization is primarily an organizational problem and upholds that organizations cannot afford to rely on learning through chance.

To clarify the notion of learning in projects, in the following I take a closer look at learning from the point view of the individuals and teams who are engaged in the process of learning (for simplicity, referred to as *learners*). In an ideal case, the learners engaged in a project (the focal project) could acquire three types of knowledge: new knowledge, existing knowledge, and institutionalized knowledge.

The new knowledge

New knowledge is gained within the project itself as a result of various project activities, such as knowledge about the requirements of new customer group or knowledge about technical or procedural issues. The knowledge is gained mainly through active observation, experimentation and involvement in project activities. During those processes, 'the learners' observe, reflect, integrate, and conceptualize their understanding of the casual links between events (positive or negative) and outcomes, and then generate new knowledge elements, which may take the form of narratives, lessons learned, diagrams, sketches, and ideas. Thus, the knowledge elements include both tacit and explicit knowledge. The main knowledge-related risk during the process is overfocus on deliverables, leaving little time to reflect on and document lessons learned. In addition, due to the autonomous nature of project activities, individuals or teams may develop a knowledge silo, such that their knowledge is not available to the wider organization, which in turn reduces the possibilities of wider sharing of the knowledge elements. A further risk is that the individuals involved will simply fail to connect and integrate their individual knowledge bases because they each have their own perception of experience (Wenger 1998).

Existing knowledge from previous projects

Organizations have an existing knowledge base (both tacit and explicit knowledge), which comprises knowledge gained by other learners from previous projects or from ongoing projects. Let us assume that this knowledge is accessible to the learners in the focal project through some kind of repository or through various forms of social networks. The knowledge is potentially helpful for avoiding the risks of repeating earlier mistakes or 'reinventing the wheel'. However, the use of the knowledge is not simple and some knowledge-related risks are involved. The learners should first sort out the huge amount of knowledge, evaluate the relevance and usefulness of the information, and then select what is relevant for their own situation and disregard the other knowledge. Thereafter, they have to make sense of the selected knowledge and integrate it into what they already know or have experienced, which involves risks. Only then will the learners be able to apply the knowledge in their own context, which is where learning may fail (Keegan and Turner 2001, Williams 2007, Duhon and Elias 2008).

Institutionalized knowledge

Institutionalized knowledge includes knowledge about, for example, organizational assets, processes, and templates (Davenport and Prusak 1998). For simplicity, it can be assumed that institutionalized knowledge is accessible to learners in the focal project, where they will need to understand, integrate and apply the knowledge in timely fashion. The knowledge-related risks identified in the two preceding sections apply to institutionalized knowledge.

Thus, any analysis of project learning may benefit from a multilevel approach, given a variety of contexts: generation of new knowledge as well as the accumulation of learning may take place within project teams, between project teams, at the level of the firm, and certainly also between firms (Sydow et al. 2004). This may suggest that learners in the focal project are engaged in two intertwined activities:

1. active experimentation, reflection, accumulation of knowledge, and probably capture of knowledge within the focal project, a type of learning denoted variously as learning within projects (Williams 2007), intra-project learning (Kotnour 2000), project-based learning (Ayas and Zeniuk 2001), or simply project learning (Newell and Edelman 2008)
2. deliberate seeking and utilization of knowledge and experience from other individuals, other projects (even outside the organization), from completed projects, or from the organization's assets base to support the learners' learning process. This dimension of learning is denoted variously as learning between projects (Hartmann and Dorée 2015), inter-project learning (Prencipe and Tell 2001) or cross-project learning (Newell and Edelman 2008).

The framework used throughout this book is shown in Figure 5. The framework does not deal with organizational learning in general, but rather focuses on learning within projects (intra-project learning) and between projects (inter-project learning). Intra-project and inter-project learning are two critical components in the process of building effective learning capability in any project-based organization (Sense 2011).

Figure 5 Framework of the study: Inter and Intra-project learning

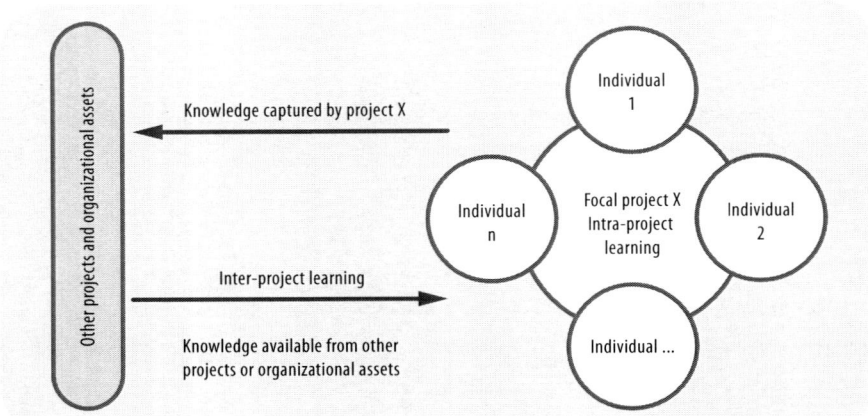

3.1 Intra-project learning

Intra-project learning takes place when individuals are given an opportunity to experiment, reflect and accumulate knowledge individually or in groups while engaged in a project. Intra-project learning takes advantage of knowledge gained from experimentation and problem-solving. This is primarily a learning-by-doing approach and is a part of the experiential type of learning (Turner et al. 2000, Zollo and Winter 2002). Experiential learning is defined by Kolb (1984, p. 21) as follows:

> the process whereby knowledge is created through transformation of experience.

Kolb's experiential learning cycle has become a well-accepted model to explain the role of experience in learning, as shown in Figure 6.

Kolb's model demonstrates that experience alone is not enough to ensure learning. If individuals want to learn from experience, they have to purposefully reflect on it (Busby 1999b). Therefore, reflection is needed to conceptualize such experiences as insights. Only then can the new insights be shared or applied and tested in new situations, which in turn will lead to new experiences and ideally the cycle will be repeated.

Figure 6 Experiential learning (Kolb 1984, p. 21)

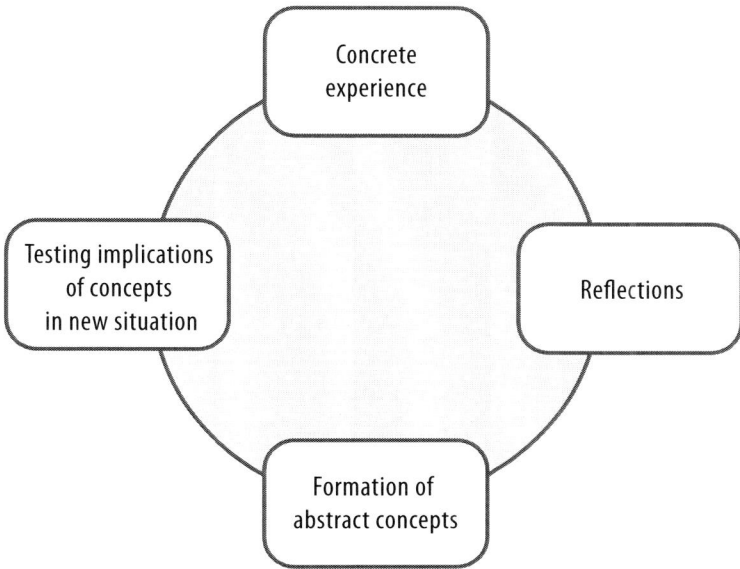

Kolb's model is a reflection–action based model and is useful for explaining how individuals learns through experience. However, transforming individual experiences into accumulated concepts and insights that are potentially useful for the focal project requires more effort (Boud and Walker 1998). Sense (2011) suggests that the transformation requires organizational practices and an organizational culture that stimulate individuals to learn while they work and work while they learn in a more deliberate and systematic way. Kotnour (2000) suggests further that if every step in the project management process is viewed from a learning perspective (e.g. by applying the process of 'plan, do, study, act'), project management process will be able to serve as the basis for the production and sharing of knowledge for the project team. Furthermore, Ayas (1996) argues that learning within a project does not happen naturally and has to be integrated into core organizational processes because it requires attention, commitment and continuous investment of resources. Although intra-project learning in project-based organizations can affect many different outcomes, three knowledge domains seem particularly noteworthy (van Donk and Riezebos 2005), and comprise knowledge about the following:

- Suppliers, contractors, regulators, competitors, customer base, market situation, customer preferences, internal relationships, and relationships with partners. This type of knowledge can be described as knowledge *about* the context of projects in which the organization operates.
- Products and technologies. This type of knowledge provides information about the strengths or limitations of the products, services and technologies used and can be an important input for risk assessment processes or design processes in future projects.
- Procedural knowledge (know-how and know-why). This is perhaps the most difficult type of knowledge to acquire and convey. It is tacit knowledge, process-oriented and subject to different interpretations.

Thus, intra-project learning requires practices and a culture that encourage individuals to use time to reflect *individually as well as collectively* on their own experiences (Cavaleri and Fearon 2000). These useful insights can then be used in new situations and the learning cycle will ideally be repeated when the new insights are tested or applied in new situations, as illustrated in Figure 7.

Figure 7 shows intra-project learning on a group level takes place through the integration of individuals' reflections (Elkjaer 2003). The reflections include fragments of *knowledge elements* that can be in the form of, for example, lessons learned, narratives, cases, rules, and ideas (Liebowitz 2005).

Learning can be accelerated by providing individuals with platforms for interacting and sharing the knowledge-element. The platforms may include using perspective and retrospective methods, such as performing various types of project reviews (Kransdorff 1996, Busby 1999b, Von Zedtwitz 2002, Atkinson et al. 2006, Koners and Goffin 2007, Williams 2007, Anbari et al. 2008, Shokri-Ghasabeh and Chileshe 2014). The main task in the reviews is determining what should be done in order to perform better in the next phase or stage of the project, bearing in mind what the team has already experienced. This type of review can be compared with single-loop learning (Argyris 1977). As suggested earlier in subchapter 2.1, in single-loop learning, actions are taken to keep the performance within norms, which results in eliminating the symptoms without focusing on the real sources of the problems.

Other learning methods are less formal and more suited for learning tacit knowledge, such as direct interaction through personal networks (Zollo and

Figure 7 Intra-project learning summarized

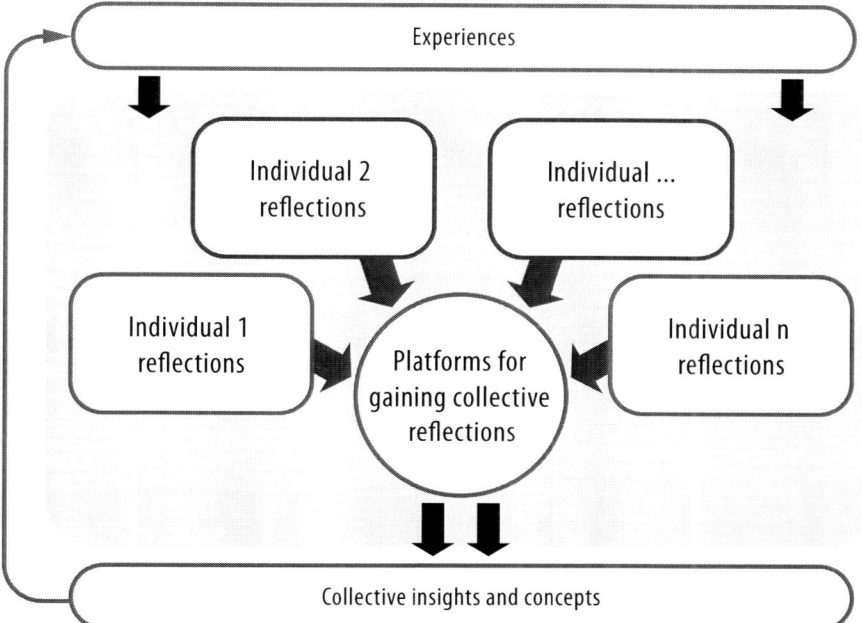

Winter 2002, Newell and Edelman 2008). Direct interaction methods requires good planning of physical space to allow for knowledge sharing. Koskinen et al. (2003) suggest that physical space can influence the type of interaction that occurs within and among people in a project by allowing for frequent interactions among project team members. Such proximity tends to elevate interpersonal collaboration, while also creating accessibility to tacit knowledge held by other team members.

Establishing community of practices can contribute to learning within projects (Wenger 1998, Sense and Antoni 2003). For example, Hara and Schwen (2006) suggest that communities of practice provide an informal learning environment in which experienced members of the community interact with each other and share their experiences of being in a particular profession, as well as learn from each other.

The most important findings from visiting the literature on intra-project learning can be summarized as follows:

- New knowledge is created through experimentation and problem solving. The new knowledge can be an idea, a lesson learned, a story, an explanation, a drawing, or an idea, all of which provide useful insights that can contribute to individuals' competency development.
- At a project level, individual experiences can be integrated by providing individuals with formal and informal platforms for sharing and integrating their insights. When the collective insights are applied in new situations, they form the basis for new experiences.

3.2 Agile approaches to intra-project learning

Intra-project learning emphasizes the importance of continuous reflection and sharing in order to continuously improve project performance and learning. I argue that some of the challenges associated with improving intra-project learning could be attributed to the nature of the project life cycle models adopted in the majority of project-based organizations. In most heavy engineering projects such as shipbuilding, oil and gas, construction, and highways, the project life cycle models are based on the predictive life cycle models (Hussein 2018).

A predictive life cycle model (also called a plan-driven model or waterfall model) follows several predefined milestones or phases. The phases are often sequential but can overlap if there is a need to fast-track the project. A typical predictive project life cycle consists more or less of the following stages:

- Starting the project or the initiation stage – includes the development of the initial goal and specifications. In this phase it is important to set the stage of the project and establish alignment with project goal and objectives.
- Organizing and preparing (planning stage) – all detailed specifications, schedules and plans are developed. Project plan and defining both responsibility and accountability are keywords during this stage.
- Execution and control – the actual work of the project is done. Results are delivered and eventual corrective actions are applied. Progress reporting, follow-up and maintaining alignment are key factors.
- Close-out or handing over – results are transferred to the customer, resources reassigned, and the project is terminated.

Typically, reflections on learning, discussing improvement potentials and other knowledge-related activities are performed and documented at the end of each phase or at completion in a plan-driven model (retrospective thinking). This method is based on the assumption that individuals and teams will be given enough time for reflection and abstracting between the milestones. However, in practice, the balancing act between adhering to a pre-defined project plan, producing deliverables, reflection, and learning is far from easy to achieve and maintain. Individuals and teams often perform under sustained pressure to deliver (time pressure) and may abandon practices related to reflection and learning, in turn leading to diminished opportunities for knowledge sharing, learning, and reflection (Babb et al. 2014). Thus, the predictive life cycle model has inherent key characteristics that could impact learning activities:

- An implicit assumption in the model is that the team assigned to the project has more or less all the competencies needed for all planning, execution and follow-up activities. In reality, this is rarely the case. The model provides little room for individuals and teams to explore the existing knowledge base either within the organization or outside it in search of available and relevant knowledge assets and resources to aid various project activities.
- The model implies that ability to influence or make changes to the scope or specifications decreases over the time because the costs of changes increase during the life of the project. Furthermore, making any changes requires extensive negotiations with the client and changes to the contract terms. In turn, this puts enormous pressure on individuals and teams, and can prevent them from taking full advantage of the knowledge gained during the project to implement changes or to adapt the specifications as a result of learning. Therefore, a typical restrictive no-change approach, such as adopted in many project-based organizations to keep to costs and schedule, could impact learning adversely.
- The model has a strong focus on documentation at the end of each stage as a precondition to proceed to the next stage that is far more than focusing on validating the value of the documentation for future project learning. Documentation is produced to fulfil a requirement rather than to learn or to improve learning. Sense (2011) suggests that learning by writing and rewriting could contribute to better knowledge sharing and thus improve

project learning. In addition, documentation of tacit knowledge requires careful and collective articulation and codification of the tacit knowledge gained during the project, which is not an easy task.

Adaptive life cycle models

By contrast, adaptive life cycle models are lightweight processes that employ short incremental cycles. Adaptive life cycle models put less emphasis on up-front plans and strict control, and such models rely more on informal collaboration, coordination and learning (Dybå et al. 2014). Also, adaptive life cycle models rely on the active involvement of the various stakeholders in each increment. Moreover, such models rely heavily on a team's tacit knowledge as opposed to documentation. In an adaptive life cycle model, the deliverables are delivered over multiple increments and the scope of each increment is only defined at the beginning of that increment).

The adaptive life cycle approach provides individuals, teams and other stakeholders with greater ability to influence project development throughout its entire life cycle. A further advantage of applying adaptive models is that the evaluation is carried out on a regular basis after each increment (Siddique and Hussein 2016, Siddique and Hussein 2019). The scope of the work in each increment is limited and therefore the achievement of results after each increment can be easily measured. Possibly more significantly, the assessment and evaluation are performed jointly. The regular and continual evaluation in adaptive life cycle models offers several advantages over the predictive life cycle models, particularly with regard to learning, such as the following:

- Continuous measurement of the project status brings all individuals, teams, and other stakeholders together, thus creating a broader and inclusive arena for reflections and evaluations.
- The incremental nature of adaptive models allows for more instances of reflections before and after actions taken, which increases opportunities for knowledge discovery and sharing within the team, and may contribute to better integration of the knowledge elements held by individuals.

3.3 Inter-project learning

In addition to working with tasks in hands, and generating and integrating knowledge, individuals and teams engage in two other parallel activities:

1. Knowledge reuse, drawing on knowledge gained from previous projects or stored as organizational assets or rules.
2. Knowledge dissemination to ongoing projects or future projects.

Figure 8 Inter-project learning

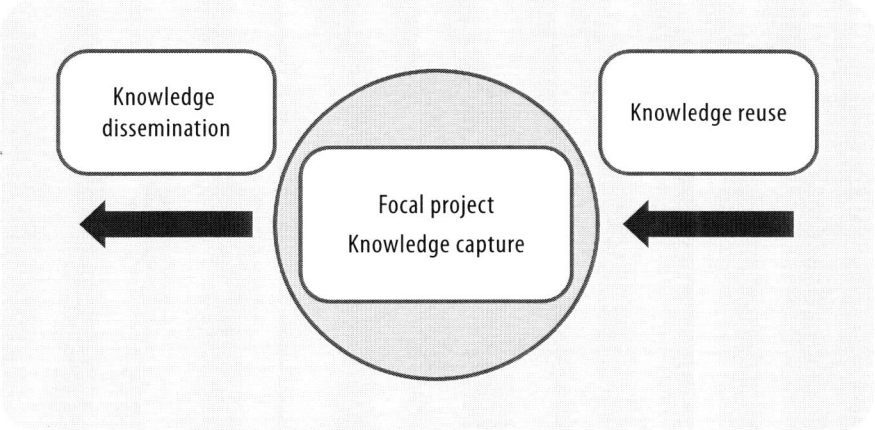

Compared to intra-project learning, inter-project learning has more to do with *deliberate* capture, dissemination and reuse of knowledge across projects in the organization in order to avoid repeating earlier mistakes, to improve performance or to avoid 'reinventing the wheel' (Figure 8). Inter-project learning is about making the knowledge gained from the focal project available for the next project and reusing effectively the available knowledge in the organization. The achievement of this objective has been debated in the organizational learning literature (e.g. Sydow et al. 2004). A variety of strategies and means exist for knowledge transfer. One such strategy is based on the cognitive perspective of learning. The cognitive view assume that knowledge is a transferable commodity that can be extracted from individuals, stored in repositories and later transferred to other individuals (Gherardi and Nicolini 2000). Hartmann and Dorée (2015)

refer to this view as the sender–receiver approach to learning, which depends on the characteristics of the sender unit, the receiving unit, the relationship between sender and receiver, and the knowledge transferred, as shown in Figure 9.

Figure 9 Knowledge transformation, cognitive view

Cognitive view

Figure 9 indicates that many barriers have to be overcome for the sender–receiver model to have any value for learning. Such barriers are rooted in the nature of the procedural knowledge captured in projects. This type of knowledge cannot be documented and shared in the same way as information stored in reports, databases or prototypes. Polanyi (1966, p. 4) refers to this phenomenon as 'tacit knowledge' and describes the underlying problem of organizations as follows: 'We know more than we can tell.' An example of tacit knowledge is the ability to ride a bicycle without having the slightest idea of the bodily processes involved (Koskinen et al. 2003).

Despite increasing awareness of the difference between tacit and explicit knowledge, it is still challenging (if possible at all) to convert tacit knowledge into explicit knowledge so that it can be shared by the entire organization. In addition, tacit knowledge undergoes many transformations before it is learned or transferred between projects or to the organizational level (Michell and McKenzie 2017). Initially, tacit knowledge has to be made explicit (codified) for other individuals to recognize it or act upon it. Other individuals have to reconcile the new knowledge with what they already know, apply it and embed it in praxis (Leonard and Swap 2005). For the learning to become institutionalized or used by other groups, groups or individuals must understand what the original learners understood and then embed that understanding in possibly different contexts (Crossan et al. 1999). Each transformation requires different conditions in order to connect senders and learners and to facilitate recognition and/or acceptance of knowledge utility.

The transformations can be further explained by the conceptual model developed by Nonaka (1991) and shown in Figure 10, and that describes how explicit and tacit knowledge are generated, transferred and recreated in organizations. The model distinguishes between four modes of knowledge transformation: socialization, externalization, combination, and internalization (SECI).

Figure 10 The SECI model (Nonaka and Takeuchi 1995)

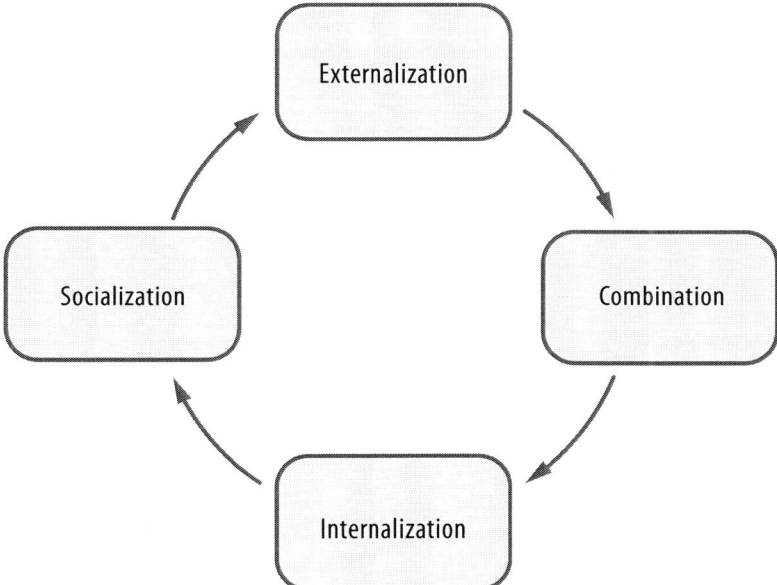

Socialization takes place at the level of individuals and it results in the sharing of tacit knowledge among the individuals through observation, mentoring and participation in social networks. In practice, socialization involves sharing knowledge through physical proximity. The process of acquiring knowledge is largely supported through direct interaction between individuals. Koskinen et al. (2003) suggested that proximity has a positive effect on tacit knowledge transference. However, they recognize that sharing and applying learning on the basis of tacit knowledge can occur only when all people involved are present and therefore such knowledge cannot be easily utilized by the overall organization or by future projects (Basten and Haamann 2018).

Externalization is the transformation of tacit knowledge into explicit knowledge through articulation by using words, figurative language (such as metaphors, analogies or narratives) and visuals. As a mode of knowledge, externalization requires conversion of tacit knowledge into comprehensible codes, symbols and assets that can be understood by others. In practice, externalization requires perspective-making, which in turn requires individuals and teams to articulate and codify the tacit knowledge in order to convert it into explicit insights that can be used by others in new situations.

Combination is the process of integrating explicit knowledge into a larger knowledge system. Explicit knowledge is transformed into more complex knowledge by *connecting* explicit knowledge elements held by different individuals or groups. Knowledge repositories are often used as storage for explicit knowledge and documents that are accessible for individuals and organizations. However, the effectiveness of such repositories is still in question: Newell et al. (2006) examined 13 projects to assess the effectiveness of ICT-based repositories and found that ICT-based strategies for capturing and transferring knowledge across projects were implemented widely but were not particularly useful.

Internalization is the process of embedding explicit knowledge in tacit knowledge. In practice, internalization requires perspective-taking and actualization of the explicit knowledge through, for example, practice, simulations and training programmes to help the individuals to apply the newly acquired knowledge in new situations and thus generate new experiences.

Social constructivist view

Acquired procedural knowledge undergoes many transformations, has to pass the test of time, and then be received, understood and applied by others in entirely different contexts, which may reduce the chances of effective inter-project learning. Therefore, the cognitive view has been challenged by the social constructivist view of learning, which suggests that learning not only takes place in the human mind and can be codified and transferred, but also occurs through the interaction of people during their day-to-day activities and as an ongoing social accomplishment (Orlikowski 2006). From this perspective, knowledge transfer between projects in which practices are not connected is impossible.

From the social constructivist point of view, inter-project learning takes place by getting individuals from different projects to sit together, analyse situations, and exchange their stories and narratives. Only then can the knowledge utility have value for the receivers of knowledge. In this view, knowledge is differentiated from knowing (Araujo 1998).

Furthermore, the social constructivist view suggests that knowing, practice and the context cannot be separated and therefore the only way to transfer knowledge is through the social interaction of individuals. Thus, in this perspective, individuals are the active carriers of knowledge – they are the knowers.

In order to support inter-project learning within the social constructivist perspective, researchers have proposed that individuals should be moved between projects to ensure the transference of knowledge between projects (project-to-project rotations) (Bartsch et al. 2013, Aerts et al. 2017). Bennett (2003) suggests that enabling staff to work in different areas of the organization through job rotation can contribute to knowledge exploitation by spreading individuals' expertise more widely within the organization. In addition, job rotation can contribute to the development of social and individual human capital by establishing and developing new relationships across the organization.

However, the constructivist view fails to take into consideration that opportunities for social interaction can occur between ongoing projects and is hardly applicable when there is a tangible time-lag between projects or when individuals leave their positions after completing the project. As shown in Chapter 1, the practice of having temporary positions in projects is quite widespread. The knowledge gained by the holders of the temporary positions might be lost after they have completed their tasks and leave the organization (Schindler and Eppler 2003, Lindner and Wald 2011). Moreover, new human encounters take place whenever a new project is started, which may increase the barriers to learning from the previous experiences of others. A further consideration is that it is not always feasible to move individuals between projects due to practical considerations and high turn-over of employees (Song and Parry 1997, Bennett 2003, Santos et al. 2016).

Intra project learning requires learning practices and attitudes that encourage individuals to spend time on experimentation and reflection, both individually as well as collectively through suitable platforms to support reflections and knowledge accumulation and to develop useful insights. By contrast, inter-project learning requires organizational learning practices and attitudes that support capture, dissemination and the reuse of the knowledge to improve the project performance and to avoid repetition of earlier mistakes.

Within the cognitive perspective, identifying lessons learned through, for example, post-project reviews has emerged as a powerful tool for identifying lessons learned that are applicable to future projects or for the wider organization (Shokri-Ghasabeh and Chileshe 2014, Hartmann and Dorée 2015, McClory et al. 2017). For example, Ekrot et al. (2016) show that the establishment of a formal lessons-learned process is positively related to the retention of project management competence.

3.4 What is a lesson learned?

It is not straightforward to define the meaning of a lesson learned. In simple terms, a lesson learned is an expression of a complex knowledge-sharing process (Milton 2010). The lessons-learned process refers to the process of capturing the knowledge gained from projects and work activities, and then transferring that knowledge beyond the team to be reused by other projects and even by other organizations (Williams 2007). Hence, the lessons-learned process may be thought of as an attempt to integrate and cement together intra-project and inter-project learning activities.

In the literature on lessons learned the process is described as comprising mainly three subprocesses:

1. capturing (e.g. through various forms of project reviews)
2. transfer (e.g. from a knowledge repository)
3. reuse in future projects.

Lessons are considered to be intellectual assets that, if used correctly, can create value (Carrillo et al. 2013). The main goal of a lessons learned process is to aid organizations to learn from project experiences by converting the experiences into recommendations for improvements of some kind (NATO 2011). Accordingly, some authors distinguish between lessons identified and lessons learned (Weber et al. 2001).

There are several definitions of lessons learned. For example, Schindler and Eppler (2003, p. 220) state that lessons learned as:

> key *project experiences* which have a certain general business relevance for future projects. They have been validated by a project team and represent a consensus on a *key insight* that should be considered in future projects.

This definition implies that lessons learned represent consensus and the need for a method to verify lessons for their *applicability* for future projects.

Another definition for lessons learned is currently used by American, European, and Japanese space agencies (Secchi et al. 1999, p. 58):

> A lesson is knowledge or understanding gained by experience. The experience may be positive, as in a successful test, mission, exercise, or workshop, or negative, as in a mishap or failure. Successes and failures are both considered sources of lessons. A lesson must be significant in that it has a real or assumed impact on operations; valid in that is factually and technically correct; and applicable in that it identifies a specific design, process, or decision that reduces or eliminates the potential for failures a mishap, or reinforces a positive result.

This definition implies the need to verify lessons for correctness, usefulness and applicability.

3.5 The role of post-project reviews

Post-project reviews aim to capture knowledge that can enhance future project work and thus they differ from milestone reviews or ad-hoc lessons-learned sessions that aim at improving the performance of the focal project. Therefore, post-project reviews can be compared with double-loop learning because they provides a basis for questioning the methods used, such as leadership style, working culture, and values and norms (Von Zedtwitz 2002). Collier et al. (1996) have suggested a model for conducting post-project reviews that uses surveys consisting of six stages, of which the final stage is to identify an organic link between the identified lessons and future projects. In post-project reviews, the emphasis is on the following (Koners and Goffin 2007, Milton 2010, Project Management Institute 2013):

- Learning from success. This is done by having the project team reflect on the factors that have contributed to the project success, as well as what could have been done differently to achieve better results. Learning from success is difficult. Successes generally confirm prior expectancies and do not raise any concerns for immediate change. Thus, if it is desirable for learners to draw lessons from their successes, Ellis and Davidi (2005) suggest that they should be induced accordingly. By attracting learners' attention not only to the obvious failed aspects of their activity but also to successful stories or decisions, it is possible to intensify their epistemic activity, trigger their motivation to revise their knowledge structures, and ultimately improve their performance.

- Learning from failure. This includes learning from the challenges that the project had to deal with, as well as the root causes and consequences of those challenges. In addition, learning from failure includes elaborating on how the project has managed the problems and what was the outcome of these actions. Edmondson (2011) argues that learning from organizational failures is anything but straightforward. She emphasizes that organizations need better ways to go beyond lessons that are superficial or self-serving, as well as the importance of phycological safety and a no-blame culture as a precondition for learning from failure. By contrast, Busby (1999b) makes a different argument and suggests that the main barriers to learning from failure may be attributed to the reluctance of individual team members to blame other team members or their direct superiors. Thus, there is tendency to examine the consequence of problems rather than the causes of problems.

From an organizational learning perspective (Argyris 1977), mapping failure and success is important and could lead to the following:

- Understanding the root causes of the mismatch between outcome and objectives, and identifying measures or actions to prevent or eliminate those causes
- Understanding the root causes of success and taking measure that enforce the applications of those causes in future projects (single-loop learning)
- An empirical basis for questioning the methods used, such as leadership style, working culture, and values and norms (double-loop learning).

However, retrospectives methods such as post-project reviews have several shortcomings (Busby 1999b, Von Zedtwitz 2002, Kotnour and Vergopia 2005, Koners and Goffin 2007, Anbari et al. 2008). Post-project reviews, as the name implies, take place after completing of the project and therefore there is always a time difference between the time of gaining an experience and the time of capturing this experience. Therefore, retrospectives methods such as post-project reviews are based on memory, and there is a risk that memory bias, selective memory and ambivalent experiences in projects can override potentially important and valuable information for future use (Von Zedtwitz 2002). In addition, post-project reviews require guided reflections and allocated time to discuss the root causes of problems, and revisions are required to validate the relevance and applicability of the lessons learned for future projects or for organizational learning.

3.6 Novel approaches to support knowledge sharing

In recent years a growing number of organizations have implemented various forms of social media applications to facilitate knowledge exchange within their organization (Moskaliuk and Kimmerle 2009, Jarrahi and Sawyer 2013, Behringer and Sassenberg 2015, Ellison et al. 2015, Gaál et al. 2015). For example, Grace (2009) shows that many organizations such as IBM, General Electric, Procter & Gamble, Shell, and Airbus have abandoned cumbersome knowledge management repositories in favour of applications such as blogs, wikis and other social software applications. She points to the key features of wikis as an example that embodies the knowledge-sharing dream of an organization whereby a group of its members voluntarily and unselfishly collaborates and creates knowledge, and works towards a common goal to benefit the organization (Grace 2009).

Leonardi (2017) argues that although there are differences between various social media applications, they have at least two underlying affordances in common. First, they are leaky, meaning that they make individual's communications with each other visible to third parties. Second, those communications persist over time as threads that reflect the context in which they emerged. The result of the affordances is that communication about routine work matters between people can, by design, leak from the channel of communication and into other peoples' streams of awareness. Typical modes of mediated communication used in organizations such as email, instant messaging, and memos do not have this leaky property.

Pirkkalainen and Pawlowski (2014) argue that although using social media applications has enormous implications for the management dynamics with respect to organizational knowledge, there are several obstacles to overcome. For example, Behringer and Sassenberg (2015) argue that motivation and willingness to use new social media applications for knowledge sharing and knowledge seeking is proportional to both the perceived usefulness of these applications and the experience of social media use. They found stronger intentions to contribute knowledge among individuals with more social media experience, whereas knowledge-seeking intentions were not related to experience but mainly related to the age of the knowledge seekers.

Similarly, Matschke et al. (2014) argue that it is just in an ideal world that members of online communities are enthusiastic about knowledge sharing and highly motivated. They found that time and effort requirements were the strongest factors that hindered contributions to the online communities. Furthermore, Matschke et al. (2014) point to internal motivation as the strongest factor supporting participation in such communities.

Paroutis and Al Saleh (2009) suggest that outcome expectations, perceived organizational support, and trust are key determinants for using social media tools in knowledge sharing. They further highlight several managerial implications from their study. First, they recommend that top management should take an active leadership role in introducing online technologies, communicating their benefits and articulating how they fit into the organization's strategy for knowledge management, and ultimately how they could help in the achievement of organizational objectives. It is equally important to provide the necessary training and to avoid mandating or enforcing knowledge sharing using the new technologies. Furthermore, rewards in the form of recognition are critical for encouraging knowledge sharing on electronic platforms.

4 Study contributions

Despite the environmental concerns about oil and gas exploration and related development activities on the Norwegian continental shelf, the petroleum industry plays a vital role in the Norwegian economy and the prosperity of the Norwegian people. Since oil and gas production started on the Norwegian continental shelf in the early1970s, petroleum activities have contributed to more than NOK 14,600 billion (2019) to Norway's GDP (Norwegianpetroleum 2020). This figure does not include the contributions from other services and industries related to petroleum activities.

The total net cash flow from the petroleum industry in 2019 was NOK 257 billion (Norwegianpetroleum 2020). This makes Norway's petroleum industry the largest and most important sector of Norway's economy measured in terms of value added, government revenues, investments, and export value (Figure 11).

Figure 11 Contribution of the petroleum sector in Norway (Norwegianpetroleum 2020)

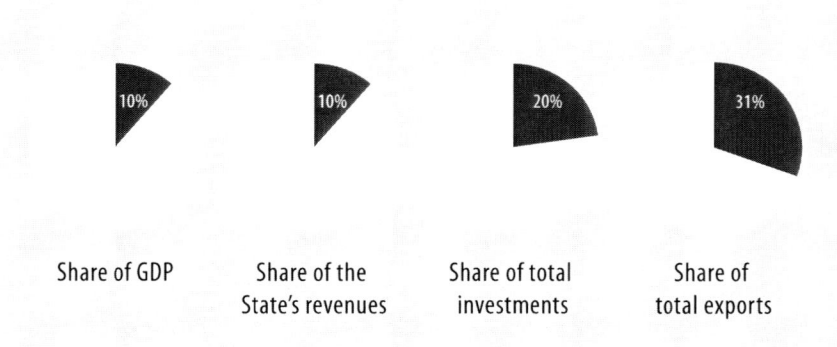

Most projects in the oil and gas industry require huge investments. As an example, the scope of investments in the further development of the Johan Sverdrup field alone, approved by the Norwegian Parliament (Storting), is currently NOK 141 billion (Norwegianpetroleum 2020). Very few industrial projects on the mainland can compare with the offshore projects in terms of investment size, revenues or export value. Offshore projects are megaprojects and are characterized by a significant number of interfaces, interdependencies, complexity, and risks, some of which are strategic and must be managed at a level above the project team (Jergeas 2008). In addition, most oil fields are owned by multiple licensees, comprise several independent activities, and require vast number of suppliers, contractors, subcontractors and consultants. Many offshore development projects on the Norwegian continental shelf have experienced delays and large cost overruns in recent years. In 2013, the Norwegian Petroleum Directorate issued a report containing an assessment of the status of oil and gas projects in Norway (Alveberg and Melberg 2013). The authors of the report suggest that from looking at all projects, the increase in relation to plans for development and operation (PDOs)/plans for installation and operation (PIO) was more than NOK 49 billion. This indicates that in recent years Norway's offshore projects have generally become more expensive than the unbiased estimate submitted in the PDOs/PIOs.

4.1 Research stages and research questions

In this book I explore the notion of learning in project-based organizations based on a combination of a literature study and extensive data gathered from a longitudinal case study of the Ivar Aasen oilfield development project. The brief literature review presented in preceding chapters points to the many challenges of learning in projects. In addition, the literature review emphasizes the need to recognize the magnitude of efforts that are needed in order to learn in project-based organizations, particularly the following:

- Efforts to enable individuals and teams in projects to learn from the tasks at hands through the process of experimentation, observation, reflection, conceptualization, and reuse of existing knowledge in the organization (enabling intra-project learning)

- Efforts to enable individuals and teams to share their knowledge with other individuals or with other teams, or even to the wider organization (enabling inter-project learning).

I have also shown that the two subprocesses of learning – inter-project and intra-project learning – cannot and should not be separated. Furthermore, failure to learn anything of value within a project will reduce the likelihood of any useful insights being produced for future projects. Similarly, adequate intra-project learning requires access to insights, knowledge and experiences gained from previous projects in order to create a fertile learning environment for the individuals and teams in the focal project.

In addition, this book contributes to the body of knowledge on learning in project-based organizations by exploring the efforts, both the means and the attitudes, that are needed to improve learning capabilities in projects when the projects are operating in complex and demanding contexts.

Thus far, I have shown that in inter-project learning social interactions have relevance and are effective for enabling knowledge dissemination and knowledge acquisition between individuals and ongoing projects. However, due to the temporality and cross-organizational nature of projects, social interactions have limitations with regard to achieving an institutionalized level of learning (i.e. retaining knowledge for future projects). The literature review suggests that reliance on knowledge captured in repositories or in written reports is challenging for both contributors to knowledge and receivers of knowledge.

Thus, the second contribution of this book is narrower than the first and focuses on improving the institutionalized level of learning in project-based organizations. Institutionalized learning refers to the footprints of learning from completed projects in the form of reusable knowledge elements that can be applied to improve future projects or organizational capabilities. In the following, I present the entire process for conducting post-project reviews. The main motivation behind the development this process is to enable the reuse of the lessons learned in new projects. In addition, I present the findings from several tests that were carried out to learn more about the impact of learning.

For the above-described purposes, I draw on the longitudinal case study of a megaproject from the offshore sector – the Ivar Aasen project. First and foremost, the Ivar Aasen project provides some useful insights into learning in a complex and demanding environment that is characterized by continuous changes, extreme time pressure, a multiplicity of stakeholders, tremendous financial impact, and market uncertainty. These characteristics make the project particularly interesting both to study and as a source of insights.

Data from the Ivar Aasen project were collected in three stages in the period 2015–2019 (Figure 12). Each stage had distinct research objectives:

- In the first stage in 2015, data were collected from the Ivar Aasen project in order to investigate the means and enablers that supported learning within the project. A total of 15 interviews were conducted with team members of the Ivar Aasen project. The data collected provided some useful insights into structural and cultural factors that impact learners' abilities to engage in experimentation, knowledge exploration and sharing in a complex project such as the Ivar Aasen project. The method, findings and discussions from this stage are presented in Chapter 5.
- In the second stage, in the period 2016–2017, the focus was on developing and implementing a process to identify the lessons learned that would be potentially useful for the institutionalized level of learning and have value for future projects. Therefore, the *relevance* of the lessons learned to future projects was in focus. A total of 25 interviews were conducted with key project members and the interviewers listened to the project members' stories, narratives and how they made sense of the events that occurred during the project. The method, findings and discussions of the process and the lessons learned are presented in Chapters 6 and 7.
- The third stage was undertaken when the organization was in the middle of a new project development effort and a new round of data collection was carried out in order to assess the impact of learning from the Ivar Aasen project on the new project. In addition, an assessment was made of how far

Figure 12 Research stages

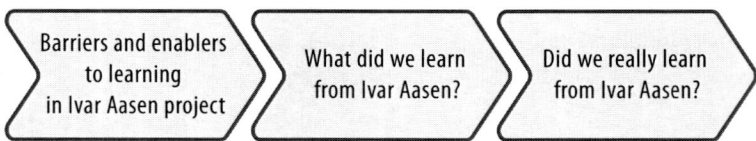

the organization was able to utilize the lessons from the Ivar Aasen project in its new project development. The findings and discussions from this stage are presented in Chapter 8.

The contributions of this book are at both the conceptual and practical levels. *Conceptually*, I show that learning and performance are not orthogonal dimensions that need to be balanced during project development. On the contrary, learning and performance are two mutually dependent parameters that have a circular relationship to the extent that various learning activities contribute to improved performance and, in turn, improved performance contributes to greater appreciation of the role of learning in the project. In order for this circular relationship to thrive, a set of attitudes and enablers should be in place. In this book, I outline and elaborate on these enablers and attitudes.

Practically, this book provides a full account of the process used to collect and analyse effectively the lessons learned, in order to ensure the reuse of the lessons in future projects. Accordingly, I use the contingency approach to identify the relevance of lessons learned to future projects. I provide deeper insights into the lessons learned from the Ivar Aasen project by focusing on learning from both failures and successes. These lessons learned could have value for readers who are interested in learning about typical challenges or gaining further insights into such challenges, the means to respond to the challenges, and the drivers for success in a demanding and complex project environment.

In addition, I present a set of postulates that could be used to evaluate the impact of learning on future projects and that were used to test the impact of learning from Ivar Aasen. The postulates cover the potential impact of learning in three clusters:

- Individual/team
- Project level
- Organizational level.

4.2 The Ivar Aasen project

Ivar Aasen field is located in the North Sea, c.175 km west of the Norwegian coastal town of Karmoey. The field is on the Utsira High, close to Lundin's field Edvard Grieg. The field was discovered in 2008 and the plan for development and operation (PDO) was approved by the Norwegian Parliament (Storting) in May 2013. It is estimated that the recoverable reserves in the Ivar Aasen field are 115.1 million barrels of oil and 33.3 billion barrels of gas. The operator of the field, Det norske, now Aker PB, was established in 2007 and the Ivar Aasen field was the first large development project for Det norske as an operator.

Due to the close proximity between Ivar Aasen field and Edvard Grieg-field, the Norwegian Petroleum Directorate suggested a tie-in arrangement between the two fields. Under this arrangement, the first-stage processing are carried out on the Ivar Aasen field and the partly processed fluids are then transported to the Edvard Grieg field for final processing and export. The total investment cost of Ivar Aasen by the end of 2015 was NOK 22,442 million and in 2016 the future investment was estimated to be NOK 3586 million. The development of the Ivar Aasen field includes a production, drilling and quarters (PDQ) platform with a steel jacket and a separate jack-up rig for drilling and completion.

Photo 1 The topside is on deck ready for sailing from Singapore (© News on Request)

Initially, the operator, Det norske, wanted an early solution, including the hiring of a floating production storage and offloading (FPSO) unit, but this solution was not accepted by the project partners. Instead, the project partners wanted a permanent platform. For Det norske, a permanent platform would have incurred financial challenges. Other partners, such as Statoil and Bayerngas Norge, considered they would be best served by having a permanent platform. After discussing the matter for a number of months, in the autumn of 2011 Det norske agreed to having a permanent platform.

By the end of 2011, Lundin, the operator of the nearby Edvard Grieg field, suggested an alternative to the development proposal, whereby the Ivar Aasen field would be coordinated with the Edvard Grieg field development, and the hydrocarbons from the Ivar Aasen field would be processed at the Edvard Grieg field. Lundin managed to convince the Norwegian Petroleum Directorate to adopt its concept.

The consequence of the early conceptual change was that a coordinated development agreement on the development of the Edvard Grieg field had to be negotiated. Among other matters, the agreement regulated the production capacity of the Ivar Aasen field, which was permitted to have a limited capacity in the first three years of production before being granted permission to produce at full capacity. The coordinated development cost the Ivar Aasen partnership a one-time payment for various modifications of the facilities at the Edvard Grieg field. Moreover, the Ivar Aasen platform became a simpler platform. Another important consequence of the coordinated development was that it gave Det norske an opportunity to start production before the end of 2016. The management in Det norske regarded the coordinated development with Edvard Grieg as an opportunity, since the investment costs were significantly lower. Additionally, Det norske was able to start production earlier. Thus, the development was seen as a positive opportunity despite the fact that negotiations with the operator of Edvard Grieg field Lundin were uneasy.

In the final phase of the work on the plan for development and operation (PDO), a new situation emerged: the geological interpretations indicated that parts of the Ivar Aasen field could extend into a neighbouring license, which was operated by Wintershall. Wintershall had decided to drill an exploration well near the limit of the area covered by the license and discovered oil. The Norwegian Petroleum Directorate concluded that the discovery was part of the Ivar Aasen deposit. Much effort was put into reaching an agreement on the size and distribution of the additional resources. The involved parties were obliged to submit an update on the resources and volume distribution, as well as an updated recovery plan in the summer of 2013. The significant events in the project are summarized in Table 3.

Table 3 Summary: significant events in the project

Coordinated development with the Edvard Grieg field and regulated production capacity, resulted in the following for the Ivar Aasen project:

§ Less complicated platform and fewer investment costs
§ Greater requirements for coordination with Edvard Grieg field
§ A number of new technical requirements and stricter requirements from operator of Edvard Grieg field (Lundin) in order to complete the planned coordination between the Ivar Aasen and Edvard Grieg fields
§ Production could start at the Ivar Aasen field (i.e. the first oil) in the fourth quarter of 2016

New discovery in the area covered by the neighbouring license:

§ New round of negotiations to agree on the allocation of resources, unitization agreement, and an updated recovery plan
§ Higher production capacity and longer life span

4.3 Contracts

Det norske understood quite early that it had to base the implementation of the project on engineering, procurement and construction (EPC) contracts. This decision was also made because the operator did not have the capacity or resources to do the EPC on its own. Additionally, the market situation was instrumental in the decision to select EPC contracts in the Ivar Aasen project. Not all of the potential suppliers were in favour of working for a small newcomer such as Det norske. This might have been the first lesson learned: *in a hot market the operator did not get to choose and has to make important decisions based on the context of the project*. It was therefore decided to have EPC contracts for the three largest deliveries: topside, jacket, and SURF (subsea umbilicals, risers and flowlines).

In addition, there were verification contracts and support contracts. Hook-up and commissioning contracts were merged together in order to avoid handover at the end of the hook-up period. Furthermore, due to the market situation, the procurement strategy was to find suppliers in parallel with FEED (*Front-End*

Engineering Design) before the PDO was delivered. This strategy was implemented to ensure that the project could be completed on schedule. Later, the strategy created unrest in the ranks of the project teams and resulted in several problems, which I will return to when presenting the lessons learned. Additionally, FEED was kept at a minimum level, which in practice meant that the project underwent a lot of changes during the subsequent detailed engineering design.

The contract for the topside was the most comprehensive contract in the Ivar Aasen project. The topside weighed 13,700 tonnes and comprised multiple parts, such as installations for processing, gas compression, separation, water injection, flame towers, and measurements. The EPC contract for the topside was awarded to a Singapore-based company, SMOE (Singapore Offshore Engineering Enterprise), with Mustang as a subcontractor on the engineering side. The construction of the topside began according to plan in December 2013 and was due to be completed in March 2016.

The jacket was to be built at Arbatax in Sardinia. It was 138 metres high and was installed at a depth of 112 metres. The total weight of the piles was 14,400 tons. The contract for the jacket was awarded to Saipem, as were the transport and installation contracts (T&I). The contract stipulated that the topside would be lifted onto the Jacket in July 2016.

Photo 2 The topside is sailing away towards Ivar Aasen field (© News on Request)

Photo 3 The jacket touches the seabed (© News on Request)

The accommodation area was on seven floors, with a total area of 3300 m². It had 70 simple cabins, as well as recreational areas, changing rooms, a control room, a helicopter deck, and all other facilities necessary for running an offshore hotel. The living quarters were built in aluminium. The contract had a fixed price, but the final price was higher. The living quarters were planned and assembled by Apply Leirvik at Stord in Norway, and included the central control room for the entire Ivar Aasen field. Additionally, all heating, ventilation, and air conditioning (HVAC) equipment for the entire topside was housed in the basement of the living quarters.

4.4 Evaluation of the project

Despite all of the challenges encountered during the Ivar Aasen oilfield development project, there was a broad consensus among those who participated in the project enquiry that the project was an overall success. According to the project literature, the evaluation of projects is a difficult topic, partly because projects have many stakeholders with different subjective perspectives and partly because no standard set of indicators exists that can be used to evaluate projects. Nevertheless, there is a broad consensus in the project literature that projects are evaluated from two dimensions (de Wit 1988, Atkinson 1999, Collins and Baccarini 2004, Jugdev and Müller 2005):

- Project management success. This is measured in terms of the project's ability to satisfy health and safety requirements (H&S), time, budget, specifications, and other scope requirements. In the case of the Ivar Aasen project, the target of 'first oil' in the fourth quarter of 2016 was a dominant and important priority.
- Project success. This evaluated as the project's ability to meet stakeholders' expectations in terms of, for example, business goals, earnings, and reputation.

With regard to project management success, the findings from the longitudinal case study suggested that the Ivar Aasen project managed to satisfy the target goals overall. Some of the deliveries in the project faced strong challenges and exceeded the budget, such as engineering, package deliveries and living quarters. Other deliveries, such as jacket, topside, SURF, hook-up, and T&I were delivered within time and budget, and according to specifications.

Drilling and well operations, and petroleum technology were success stories. The various measures implemented in the two subprojects have since contributed to substantial savings that have compensated for the cost overrun of other deliveries.

With regards to the above-mentioned second dimension of project success, the findings the longitudinal case study indicated that the project organization

Photo 4 Drilling rig Maersk Interceptor (© News on Request)

Photo 5 The living quarters (© News on Request)

facilitated stable and safe operation at the facility through good recruitment of operating personnel, the involvement of operations, and the development of operating and control procedures. Furthermore, the findings suggest that the efforts related to petroleum technology changed much of the investment image in the project. It can be therefore concluded that prerequisites for project success were present in terms of production volume, net present value, and earnings.

5 Enablers of learning

As shown in Chapter 3, individuals in projects are engaged in multiple tasks with regard to learning. They learn from the tasks at hands through the process of experimentation, reflection and conceptualization. In addition, they explore and reuse existing knowledge in the organization either through their social networks or through existing knowledge repositories. In addition, they articulate, share and disseminate their own acquired knowledge among other individuals or among the wider organization. For these multiple levels of knowledge discovery, acquisition, sharing, and distribution to exist, several factors have to be in place. The purpose of this chapter is to explore further the issue of project learning, to facilitate an understanding of the factors that support individuals' ability to acquire, share, articulate, disseminate, and reuse the knowledge in demanding project environments. The Ivar Aasen project is used as an illustrative example to answer the following question:

- What factors support or inhibit learning in complex projects such as the Ivar Aasen project?

5.1 Introduction

Recent research on project learning as a subset of organizational learning has examined the barriers that limit or hinder learning within projects. Bresnen (2006) suggests that in project-based organizations the influence of the rational perspective on project management as a discipline has in turn influenced assumptions about project assignments and how they should be managed, which has impacted intra-project learning. For example, there is a rooted assumption that projects are about 'doing', with no time allocated for learning and reflection activities. Carrillo et al. (2013) indicate that lack of time for reflection is caused by deep-seated culture of not looking back, but instead looking ahead to future. A project culture of focusing only on doing and concentrating on immediate project goals does not provide space for individuals to reflect on project learnings (Wiewiora et al. 2019).

Fuller (2011) suggests that lack of time for reflection and sharing is usually one of the main barriers to learning within projects. In an study of six large organizations, Oliver and Kondal Reddy (2006) found that almost all participants emphasized that it was essential to allocate time for learning, collaborations, knowledge creation, and sharing activities within the project. In addition, the tools and techniques available to project managers are primarily designed for convergent problem-solving activities and for achieving conformance to requirements and specifications, not to question the requirements and specifications or the rules of project execution or how to learn while working on projects. Vergopia (2008) argues that project management maturity models could possibly include project reviews in their steps, but only as a process at the project close-out phase and not as a learning tool. She further explains that project management maturity models seldom mention how the knowledge derived from the review process should be disseminated for further use by the organization.

Thus far in this book I have shown that much of the debate in current project-based learning literature is centred on the best possible approach to accomplish knowledge sharing and dissemination. The cognitive approach suggests that knowledge could be articulated, codified, captured, stored, and disseminated through lessons-learned process. By contrast, the social constructivist approach suggests that knowledge and practice cannot be separated and the only way to share knowledge is through social networks. Clearly, the truth lies somewhere between the two school of thoughts, and a combination of the two approaches should yield more optimum learning results. Although I do not argue for or against cognitive approach and the social constructivist approach, I suggest that knowledge capture and dissemination through the lessons-learned process is more suitable to support knowledge reuse in future projects, provided that the lessons are reviewed and assurance is provided as to their relevance for future projects. I return to this issue later in this book, but first I take a broader look at the enablers and barriers to learning in the Ivar Aasen project. Thereafter, I discuss them in the light of the available body of knowledge on organizational learning in general and on project-based learning in particular.

5.2 Method

The data for the longitudinal study of the Ivar Aasen oilfield development project were collected by two master's students who I supervised in the spring semester in 2015. A total of 15 semi-structured individual interviews were conducted. Purposeful sampling was used to select the interviewees from the Ivar Aasen project. Interviewees were chosen from each major subproject in the Ivar Aasen project in order to make sure that data collected is representative for the entire project. The selected interviewees included senior as well as new project team members. Each interview was recorded and fully transcribed immediately after completion. Data analysis was performed using a coding approach (Robson 2011), whereby the data were coded and labelled, and codes with the same label were grouped together as a theme. The themes served as a basis for further analysis and interpretation, in line with recommendations by Robson (2011).

5.3 Findings: enablers

The purpose of the interviews was to gain insights into the interviewees' perceptions on learning and the factors that supported or inhibited learning. The findings suggested that there was a broad acknowledgment among the interviewees that the ability to learn is dependent not only on individual wishes but also on a multitude of managerial and environmental factors. A summary of the findings from the analysis of the interviews is provided in Table 4. On the basis of the findings, 10 factors were identified as important for supporting learning within the Ivar Aasen project.

Table 4 Factors that supported learning within the Ivar Aasen project

Eagerness to learn and share	Sharing of knowledge was encouraged
Psychological safety ensured	Provision of formal opportunities for learning for individuals
Open-minded attitude	Established inclusive work environment
Error tolerance	Pool of highly experienced individuals
Physical proximity and co-location of project teams	Company's size and seniority

Eagerness to learn. According to the interviewees, eagerness to learn was evidently a contributing factor that supported learning in the project. Neither the age nor seniority of individuals seemed to have a negative influence on their willingness to learn. From the interviews, it became apparent that individuals were *willing to share* their knowledge with other individuals. Experienced individuals regarded knowledge sharing as a part of their role to help less experienced individuals and try to do whatever they could to makes sure that their knowledge was passed on before they left the project:

> I have never experienced that someone is trying to keep their knowledge to themselves.

> I'm doing some mentoring on the side, for people. I find that very rewarding.

Large pool of competence. The project operated in a complex environment and many specific areas of expertise were needed for the project to be completed. The majority of the interviewees mentioned that there were highly qualified people in Det norske and therefore there was always someone with expertise in a particular field with whom they could talk. The pool of experienced individuals facilitated learning in the Ivar Aasen project:

> One benefit is that we have very competent persons. The level of competency is very high. Here, nine out of ten people are performing excellently, while at my previous workplace it was maybe one out of ten.

Open-minded attitude. The interviewees suggested that most of the people involved in the project were open to new ideas and were not stuck in their old ways of doing things, which contributed to finding better solutions and abandoning the tradition of 'that is the way we do it':

> We have a very open-minded team that is not locked in its old ways.

It emerged further from the interviews that individuals appreciated that *asking for help* would not harm their position in the organization:

> There are a lot of people with experience that can help me. […] that is extremely helpful.

The interviewees also suggested that the management had made various efforts at the beginning of the project to establish a collaborative work environment such as by team building and by encouraging people from various locations to get to know each other. This helped to creating interpersonal trust and made discussions and exchanging ideas much easier during the face-to-face meetings:

> Management arranged that everyone was introduced in the beginning. That helped a lot.

Error tolerance. The interviewees suggested that in the project there was a culture that enabled people to try new things and were not penalized for making mistakes:

> Making mistakes is a part of learning, regardless of whether one is a new employee or has thirty years of experience.

In addition, the interviewees suggested that communications with senior management were remarkably good. They pointed in particular to the ease of having direct access to senior management and the shorter communication lines, which in turn facilitated knowledge exploration. Furthermore, the company's small size at the time when the interviews were held contributed to shorter communication lines between senior management and project teams. The quality of communication was strengthened by the *physical layout* chosen for Ivar Aasen project: the layout was planned with many open spaces, coffee areas and sofas, where people could meet and talk together informally and share experiences. In addition, there were various meeting rooms of different sizes, which made it easy for people to book meetings whenever they wanted to discuss different matters, interact, and share knowledge or information with colleagues:

> One of the advantages that we have had is that we were small and agile, not too bureaucratic.

The project teams were co-located. The co-location of project teams improved the sharing of knowledge and exchange of ideas. The impact of co-location on learning seemed to be far more significant than the impact of formal processes, such as a lessons-learned repository:

> People are stimulated to share their knowledge and they have plenty of meetings, open space for informal discussion, websites, etc. that enable sharing.

Inclusive work environment. The interviewees reported that the project depended on many consultants to provide the special expertise that the company needed in the project. The consultants maintained that they did not feel they were outsiders and did not consider their situation was any different that of a permanent employee. There was a consensus among the interviewees that the management had treated everyone the same, and the consultants felt they were an integral part of the project:

> I feel like a part of the company and I am not treated otherwise because I am a consultant. Personally, I feel that I have a free position in the company. I have been here for three and a half years and have gained both responsibility and trust.

The inclusive work environment was further supported by the availability and visibility of senior management:

> There is no problem for a junior employee to go directly and talk to senior management without involving or getting permission from their supervisor.

Provision of formal opportunities for learning for individuals. The interviewees suggested that management was supportive when people wanted to attend courses and seminars:

> Management is very supportive when I want to arrange a course for my associates.

Company size and seniority. Det norske was a new organization when it started the Ivar Aasen project. Moreover, it did not have any previous experience in executing megaprojects, which might have placed limitations on inter-project learning. However, evidence from the interviewees suggested that the situation accelerated the intra-project learning activities and contributed to more institutionalized knowledge being gained. People had to learn in order to be able to establish new processes and procedures from scratch, and in turn that need accelerated the learning process and made people more eager to learn and share knowledge:

> This is a new company, [so there is] not much information to learn from. Right now, it is all in the learning phase. [The] first real project is going now.

5.4 Findings: barriers

Most of the main barriers to learning revealed by the interviews were related to dissemination activities, including issues related to the lessons-learned repository, work overload, prioritization conflicts, and lack of familiarity with process requirements and intervals (Table 5).

Table 5 Barriers to learning

Prioritization conflicts
Work overload
Lack of familiarity with process requirements and intervals
Issues related to lessons-learned repository

Prioritization conflicts. According to the interviewees, most people were aware that dissemination and registration of lessons learned was part of the scope of their work. However, more than half of the interviewees had experienced lack of time when registering what lessons-learned activities needed attention and had to prioritize other project activities. In addition the interviewees suggested that activities such as the registration of lessons learned were down-prioritized when more importance matters needed their attention.

In addition, not having enough time to register lessons learned was pointed out by interviewees. They also experienced that their co-workers sometimes did not have the necessary time for discussions. This might have been due to high workloads in the company, as many individuals were preoccupied with their tasks:

> The only problem is that people are occupied, so it is difficult to get a hold of them but if [one] is able to talk to them, then people are very open to discussions and sharing their knowledge.

Work overload. Some interviewees attributed lack of time to the fact the management had tried to make the company lean and efficient by not hiring too many people. One interviewee suggested that other companies usually had twice the number of people that Det norske had working on projects of a similar size. That had the effect that people were very busy and therefore had to focus on finishing their tasks and meeting deadlines, rather than on learning:

> I am surrounded by deadlines every day, every week. LL is something you can do tomorrow or the next week. However, I am aware that LL is something you have to work with when it is fresh. You can't wait too long, [as] then you will forget.

Lack of familiarity with process requirements and intervals. The majority of interviewees suggested that they were not aware of any formal process or procedure to hold lessons-learned workshops every six months. Many felt that there should be more focus from management on this issue and that procedures should be implemented to ensure that lessons were gathered and registered in the repository:

> There is no procedure that says how you should gather experiences or lessons learned. I just know that I have to do it.

Issues related to the lessons-learned repository. The lessons learned repository topic often came up in the interviews and more than half of the interviewees had several complaints about the repository. Assessment of the complaints about the optimum use of the lessons-learned repository revealed that some types of complaints occurred frequently. The repository seemed to be less user-friendly than expected, which was very unfortunate given that it was the primary tool for searches for relevant lessons. The registration process also appeared to be time-consuming. The overall impression from the interviews was that the lessons-learned repository needed further development and simplification. Several interviewees suggested that it would be beneficial to have some kind of lessons-learned manager who could assist in arranging lessons-learned workshops, follow-up actions related to lessons learned, and assist in the registration of lessons learned. Although most of the interviewees had attended a lesson-learned workshop, half of them had never used the repository to register, look at or search for a lesson learned.

5.5 Discussion

Many of the findings from the interviews are in line with those from previous research on the enablers for and barriers to the promotion of learning in project-based organizations. This applies in particular to the management and individuals' commitment to learning, transparency and tolerance of errors (McGill and Slocum 1993, Berwick 1996, Ahmed et al. 1999, Edmondson and Moingeon 1999, Appelbaum 2004, Al-Alawi et al. 2007, Lucas and Kline 2008, Mueller 2014, Wiewiora et al. 2014). In addition, the findings suggested that a combination of psychological safety and willingness to not stick to old habits are important enablers to learning. Edmondsen (2004) suggests that psychological safety consists of taken-for-granted beliefs about how others will respond when one puts oneself on the line, such as by asking a question, seeking feedback, reporting a mistake, or proposing a new idea (i.e. whether others will give one the benefit of the doubt). Lack of psychological safety may lead employees to believe that they will lose their status within the company if they share knowledge with others. In addition to psychological safety, the findings suggested that the interviewees were aware of the importance of having an open-minded attitude and were encouraged to do so by their peers. They were also aware of the fact that innovation is a part of their job and they did not risk being penalized if they made a mistake. The importance of encouraging employees to have an open minded attitude has been emphasized as well by McGill and Slocum (1993) and Schein (2010).

Interestingly, it emerged from the interviews that the interviewees had a major preference regarding learning, namely that learning should be facilitated by the availability of large pool of competence in the project. The findings from interviews suggest that direct approaches through personal networks were a primary tool used to share and gain knowledge, whether in meetings or in a casual way. In turn, this may suggest that there is strong reliance on expedient learning approaches using the available pool of experiences through personal contacts. Reliance on expedite learning approach is strengthened by other environmental factors such as having open spaces, co-location within the project, an inclusive work environment, and a relatively small organization.

Based on the findings, it can be suggested that the conditions for project learning in the Ivar Aasen project appeared to be in place and were facilitated by individual factors such as willingness to search and ask for help when needed. The individuals' factors were strengthened and supported by proper managerial attitudes towards learning, as reflected by the inclusive, safe and collaborative working atmosphere. The overreliance on expedient learning combined with the project team members' commitment to achieve project objectives might have contributed to less commitment to knowledge articulation through the lessons-learned system in the organization. This suggestion is in line with previous observations made by (Swan et al. 2010). In addition, the lack of training, information, and a clear methodology regarding how and when to use the lessons-learned repository had a negative impact in terms of impeding knowledge articulation and codification efforts.

5.6 Learning and continuous improvement in performance

An interesting insight that emerged from the interviews was that in a complex project such as the Ivar Aasen project, the need to cope with complexity and uncertainty contributed to greater appreciation to the impact of knowledge sharing, knowledge seeking and innovation. In addition, the findings emphasized the importance of having a pool of experienced individuals who formed a strong knowledge base within the project to support learning. Moreover, it emerged from interviews that the holders of the knowledge base were committed to sharing their knowledge and considered it their duty. The knowledge-sharing activities and willingness to explore and innovate thrived in a safe and inclusive working environment. They were further strengthened by clear indications from top management that learning was valued and supported.

In order to understand how the project teams succeeded in promoting and nurturing the attitude of appreciating and valuing both knowledge exploration and knowledge sharing to cope with complexity, I focused on the issue and the link between learning and performance in the second part of the longitudinal study, when I conducted interviews with the project leaders of each sub-project in the Ivar Aasen project to collect and classify the lessons learned from the Ivar Aasen project. However, I present the findings in this subchapter due to their relevance to the enablers and barriers to learning in complex project environments.

The second set of interviews revealed a wealth of evidence on how intentional knowledge sharing and knowledge seeking had impacted the continuous improvement of performance of various project activities in the Ivar Aasen project. Although there were many similar stories, some of the interviewees pointed to the unique efforts undertaken during both petroleum technology and drilling and well operations that suggested the importance of learning to improving performance. Drilling and well operations, as well as petroleum technology, also demonstrated a highly effective approach to creating a 'one team' and good practices were developed for the exchange of knowledge with the suppliers. In the following, I highlight the four most important measures implemented in drilling and well operations, which I believe strongly contributed to improved performance through a focus on learning.

Recognition of cohesion and interdependency between drilling and well operations on the one hand and petroleum technology on the other hand. It was clear that good collaboration, knowledge sharing, understanding of the organic interdependency, and the cohesion between drilling and well operations and petroleum technology contributed to the success of the Ivar Aasen project. Project team members from both the operations side and the technology side acknowledged that it was important to show an understanding of each other's points of view and to find the right balance between them. This required close collaboration and knowledge sharing during planning and implementation, also with the close involvement of the suppliers in the process. Also, the mutual dependency was emphasized, both practically and visually, by the way in which the drilling and well engineering employees and petroleum technology employees worked next to each other in the field, and members of the petroleum technology's management team and members of the drilling and well operations management team sat next to each other, such that they were visible to the entire organization.

Right and duty to challenge. The creation of a common culture among all team members was encouraged as a way to challenge established truths. The approach created a dynamism and a sense of ownership because the team members felt that they were involved and had their say:

> We are going to challenge … that is, an engineer is going to challenge the system higher up. A supplier should challenge us as an operator, [and] if we see that it is appropriate, we will also challenge government requirements. But it's not just a right, it's a duty.

Recognition of one's own limitations. The project organization understood its limitations and realized that it needed to learn and use the supplier's competence. This was communicated clearly and openly to the supplier, which meant that the supplier had an opportunity to influence and be an active participant in the project instead of merely waiting for orders to arrive. The situation created a completely different type of ownership and thus improved the collaboration with the supplier:

> We [the project organization] do not have the special expertise, we want their [the supplier's] assessment of how we can best get this job done.

Strong emphasis on *performance first* was a driver for daily improvement in the tasks. Suggestions for improvements from engineers in the field were entered into an experience database. The experiences were reviewed and sorted each week, and then immediately used to schedule future drilling operations. The performance-first approach in this context did not conflict with knowledge seeking or knowledge sharing, due to individuals' awareness of the tie between learning and performance:

> We that we have managed to improve … from well to well. We started at 150 metres per day. The best we have is 380 metres per day. We have saved two billion kroner [NOK].

The above findings suggested that a healthy attitude towards learning can be achieved by stimulating individuals and teams to improve their performance continually within the project. Furthermore, the findings may suggest that learning and performance are not orthogonal dimensions that need to be balanced during project development, but rather that they are two mutually dependent parameters that have circular relationship. Various learning-related activities contribute to improved performance and, in turn, improved performance contributes to greater appreciation of the role of learning in the project.

As shown in Figure 13, the circular relationship between performance and learning can be supported by promoting and nurturing the following mindsets among individuals and teams:

Figure 13 Circular relationship between learning and performance

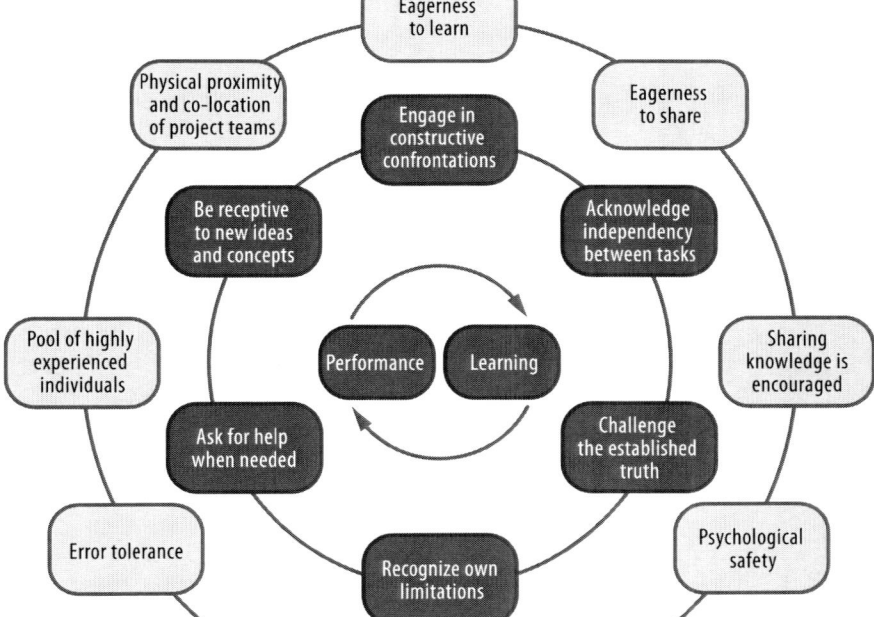

- acknowledge the interdependency between tasks within the project
- recognize own limitations
- ask for help when needed
- challenge the established norms and rules
- be receptive to new ideas and new concepts
- engage in constructive confrontations to find the right balance between differing opinions or views.

In addition, based on the findings shown in the preceding subchapter 5.3, certain contextual conditions must exist to facilitate the establishment and maintenance the above-listed attitudes. These contextual conditions are:

- Eagerness to learn and share
- Knowledge sharing encouraged
- Psychological safety ensured
- Provision formal opportunities for learning for individuals
- Established inclusive work environment
- Error tolerance
- Pool of highly experienced individuals
- Physical proximity and co-location of project teams.

6 Process for identifying lessons learned from the Ivar Aasen project

6.1 Introduction

As suggested in Chapter 5, most of the interviewees in the longitudinal study of the Ivar Aasen project believed that learning was best achieved through direct interactions with colleagues, with other project team members within the focal project or cross projects, and even outside the organization. In addition, they pointed to the difficulties associated with the search and capture of lessons learned. According to the interviewees, searching or documenting lessons learned was considered a time-consuming process that occasionally conflicted with other project priorities.

The relevance and effectiveness of social interactions for enabling knowledge dissemination and acquisitions between individuals and ongoing projects has been proven (Sense, 2011; Hartmann and Dorée, 2015). However, social interaction has limitations regarding the retention of knowledge for future projects due to the temporality of projects, the cross-organizational nature of projects, and uncertainty about the specific context of each project. Accordingly, in this chapter the focus is on improvements to the institutionalized level of learning in project-based organizations.

Previous studies have shown that capturing and formulating lessons learned from projects, for instance during post-project reviews, requires revisions, screening and verification in order to facilitate reuse in future projects (Weber et al. 2001, Davidson 2006). Lessons learned have to go through a verification process to ensure that they are well documented and not described too generally, which could otherwise can prevent their reuse (Schindler and Eppler 2003).

The general approach adopted in the longitudinal study was to associate the lessons learned with the underlying characteristics of the Ivar Aasen project and its context. The approach was based primarily on contingent thinking (Tishler et al. 1996, Balachandra and Friar 1997, Shenhar et al. 2007), which refutes the one-size fits all approach. Contingent thinking is based on the idea that management approach should change according to the circumstances. In principle, lessons learned about procedural knowledge are recommended actions in response to certain events or situations that occur during the project. It follows that by not only identifying recommendations for future projects but also explaining the situations in which the recommendations could be used, members of future projects will be able to assess the usefulness and relevance of the lessons learned. Conceptually, the findings from the study should be considered as a proof of concept: applying the contingent approach to capture lessons learned from post-project reviews could improve the reuse of the lessons learned in future projects.

6.2 The process

The scope of the post-project review process developed in this study is limited to the lessons learned that capture procedural knowledge. Hence, lessons learned regarding advanced technical issues or the choice of different types of equipment and tools are not covered. During the Ivar Aasen project, measures were taken to achieve results, to motivate and inspire people, and to encounter challenges. This type of procedural knowledge is necessary in order to establish an appropriate basis for future organizational changes or structural changes. I suggest a process consisting of the following steps:

- Use online surveys to collect factual information from individuals who have been involved in the project. Three categories of questions should be in focus:
    - Questions designed to collect information about scope of work, technological or managerial complexities, requirements, internal and external constraints, and guidelines for project execution
    - Questions designed to collect information about visible events or situations that cause concern or unrest in the project
    - Questions designed to collect information about events or situations that contribute to a positive outcome

- Based on the findings from the surveys, develop an outline of the most important characteristics of the project.
- Invite the respondents of the surveys to participate in interviews, preferably one-on-one interviews. The purpose of the interviews is to discuss and elaborate further on the project characteristics and/or the root causes of challenges, or to reflect on the specific approaches that have been implemented and discuss how they fit with the underlying characteristic of the project.
- Produce a summary of the lessons learned on how challenges have been addressed. This includes lessons learned about remedies initiated to offset or respond directly to challenges, situations and various events that occurred during the project. It is important to assess with the interviewees why the remedies were appropriate in the underlying context.
- Produce a summary of lesson learned on learning from success. This includes lessons learned about approaches used in the project and by project management, and that have helped to prevent potential hazards or have contributed to better results in general. It is important to assess with the interviewees why the remedies were appropriate in the underlying context.
- Suggest a contingent classification of the lessons learned using the outlined project characteristics, and revise the classification in collaboration with the project director.

6.3 Participant selection

Prior to data collection, it was necessary to select interviewees (Ringdal 2007). In our case, we selected 25 interviewees. The sample size seemed appropriate to achieve the purpose of the study. An overview of the responsibilities of the interviewees who provided responses to the questionnaire and/or who participated in interviews is presented in Table 6.

The interviews were conducted between November 2016 and February 2017 at Det norske's premises in Trondheim and Oslo, and each interview lasted c.30–60 minutes. All interviewees were well informed in advance about the purpose of the interview. The interviews took place in a secure and relaxed atmosphere that facilitated the openness and quality of the interviewees' responses.

Table 6 Selection of participants for interviews

Contractors	Support functions	Subproject managers	Project management
Hook-up Topside Jacket	Contracts Project control Health and Safety Communication	Edvard Grieg tie-in Package deliveries Living quarters Hook-up Drilling & well operations Jacket SURF Transport and installation (T&I) Petroleum technology (PETEK) Operations preparation Topside Platform manager	Project director Field manager CEO, Aker BP

6.4 Data collection

The data collection in the longitudinal study of the Ivar Aasen project was based on three strategies:

- Investigation into the reported lessons learned in the company's database. This gave me an opportunity to identify and gain an overview of various situations and challenges associated with the implementation of the Ivar Aasen project that had been reported on a continual basis.
- Survey questionnaire with open questions. The purpose of each questionnaire was twofold: (1) to give the respondents an opportunity to describe in their own words their experiences and reflections on key topics that study administrators considered were relevant and useful: and (2) to give the respondents the opportunity to prepare for the planned interviews. During the interviews, the respondents had an opportunity to elaborate on their answers to the questionnaires or to raise other issues about which they had been concerned. For that purpose, four different types of questionnaires were prepared:
  1. A questionnaire aimed at subproject managers of the main deliveries. This was the most comprehensive survey. It consisted of 28 open questions (see Appendix 11.1). The questions were grouped into seven main categories: work tasks, success factors, implementation frameworks, complexity, people and relationships, uncertainty, and relations with senior management and/or project management.

2. A questionnaire that focused on support functions in the Ivar Aasen project, including health and safety (H&S), communication, contracts, and project management. This questionnaire was less comprehensive than the above-mentioned questionnaire and consisted of two main categories: Success factors and relations with senior management and/or subproject managers (see Appendix 11.2).
3. A questionnaire designed for the management of Det norske and the Ivar Aasen project. This questionnaire was similarly less extensive than the first questionnaire mentioned above and consisted of challenges, success factors and overall assessment of project management effort (see Appendix 11.3).
4. A questionnaire aimed at the suppliers of the largest deliveries in the Ivar Aasen project (see Appendix 11.4).

The respondents' answers were relatively short, and shorter than expected. This might have been because they did not understand the questions, the questions were not relevant to them, or that they did not have enough time available in which to write comprehensive answers. Only a few respondents provided comprehensive answers to the questionnaires, while some did not respond to their questionnaire but agreed to be interviewed. The answers from the questionnaires were very helpful for providing an overall view of the complexity, uncertainty and main efforts with respect to the unique features of the Ivar Aasen project.

Semi-structured interviews are suitable when the aim is to obtain descriptions from study participants in a way that ensures neither an open conversation nor a closed questionnaire (Kvale and Brinkmann 2009). The relevant questionnaires were used during the interviews and used as a framework for the conversations without going through all of the questions. The interview format was intended to give the interviewees an opportunity to elaborate on their answers to their questionnaire or to express their own thoughts and reflections. Semi-structured interviews are a good tool for obtaining information about interviewees' experiences and points of view, especially when there is a need to gain deeper insights into how the interviewees have experienced their situation (Thagaard 2008).

The interviews were conducted by Torgeir Anda and me. Torgeir Anda was a consultant for Det norske from the autumn of 2014 until the work on the project was completed. Hence, he had a close relationship with the Ivar Aasen project and those who worked on it. Between us, we had sufficient knowledge and understanding of the context of the interviews. The fact that the interviews were conducted by two people with different professional perspectives was useful, both during the interviews and during the analysis, as it gave me a better understanding of the interviewee's statements and experiences. At the same time, it provided an opportunity to develop a neutral interpretation of the interviewee's experiences. Some of the interviews were conducted in the presence of a master's student from NTNU.

In order to preserve anonymity and confidentiality, the interviewees are not by name in the presentation of the findings, all quotes are anonymous, and the data collected were not made available to Det norske. During the interviews, we made audio and video recordings on mobile phones, which enabled us to spend more time focusing on the questions we asked the interviewees and their responses (Thagaard 2008). All of the recordings were then transcribed by the above-mentioned master's student to make the content of the interviews available for analysis. Thereafter, all video and audio material was deleted and the transcribed material was stored offline on a separate laptop. Transcribing is a time-consuming process but also an important part of data processing. In our case, it resulted in c.140 pages of text (c.80,000 words).

6.5 Data analysis

The data collection resulted in comprehensive data material. All transcripts were imported into Nvivo software package for coding. Six primary themes were used to encode data from the interviews. These themes were grounded in the stages of the process used:

- Characteristics of the Ivar Aasen project in terms of uncertainty, complexity and the constraints imposed on the project, and the project's criticality to the organization's success.
- Visible events and situations that caused concern or unrest in the Ivar Aasen project, which the interviewees articulated during the interviews or in their responses to the questionnaires.

- Root causes of challenges. These are possible explanations for the sources of the challenges encountered.
- Lessons learned on how challenges were addressed. These include lessons learned about remedies initiated to offset or respond directly to challenges, situations and various events that occurred along the way in the Ivar Aasen project.
- Lessons learned about drivers for success in the project. The drivers included approaches that been used in the project and by project management, and that helped to prevent potential hazards. The measures also contributed to better team collaboration, minor problems with some suppliers, and better results in general.
- Association between lessons learned and project characteristics.

6.6 Characteristics of the Ivar Aasen project

This subchapter presents the underlying conditions that governed decision-making in the project, and hence were important in order to be able to draw applicable and useful lessons learned from the project. Previous research has shown that failure to understand the unique context of a project may have adverse consequences for understanding the root causes of the problems encountered or the effectiveness of the measures taken (Chang 2002, Chan et al. 2004).

The operator company (Det norske) was a newcomer
The Ivar Aasen project was unique in many ways. Having been given the opportunity to interview many people who were involved in the project, I was left with the impression that there was an organic relationship between the operator company and the project. In many ways, the fate of operator company was dependent on the success of the Ivar Aasen project. Equally, the project was dependent on the company's ability to learn and adapt to the project needs.

The Ivar Aasen project was the first major project for Det norske as an operator. Det norske, which was established in 2007, was relative newcomer as an operator of a large oilfield and did not have a large organization when the work on the Ivar Aasen project started. From the outset, Det norske did not have all systems or processes needed to support project development. Moreover, there was no sense of team spirit when the project began.

Although Det norske's organization was fresh, there were many experienced people, yet they had not worked together as a team earlier and thus they were a new team. Furthermore, the project organization was built up simultaneously as the project evolved. The lack of human resources at start-up can be regarded as an opportunity because the operator had a unique opportunity to recruit the best human resources. However, recruitment was not an easy task because there were many other projects and activities at the time and the market for human resources was 'hot'. Therefore, the project started with almost a blank sheet.

Date for first oil
Lundin, the operator of the nearby Edvard Grieg field, suggested an alternative to the development proposal, whereby the Ivar Aasen project would be coordinated with the Edvard Grieg field development and the hydrocarbons from the Ivar Aasen field would be processed at the Edvard Grieg field. The proposed concept was duly accepted by the authorities and then the Ivar Aasen partners had to accept the decision in order to avoid postponing the project by at least one year:

> If the concept proposed by the authorities had not been accepted, the Ivar Aasen project would have been postponed by at least another year.

The consequence of the early conceptual change was that a coordinated development agreement had to be negotiated. For instance, the agreement regulated the production capacity of the Ivar Aasen field, which was permitted to have a limited capacity in the first three years of production before being granted permission to produce at full capacity. The management in Det norske saw the coordinated development with Edward Grieg field as an opportunity because the investment costs were significantly lower. Additionally, Det norske was able to start production faster. The intention was clear: to start production (i.e. 'first oil') in the fourth quarter of 2016. The date of the first oil was instrumental to many of the decisions taken later during the project.

Market situation and procurement strategy
Due to lack of internal human resources, the management in Det norske understood quite early that they had to base the implementation of the project on engineering, procurement and construction (EPC) contracts. This decision was also

made because the Det norske workforce did not have the capacity or resources to perform the EPC itself. Additionally, the market situation was influential in the decision to select EPC contracts in the Ivar Aasen project:

> A total of five major projects were out in the market at the same time.

Most of the suppliers were not in favour of working for a small newcomer such as Det norske; conversely, Det norske could not choose suppliers from the top shelf. The interviewees reported that major suppliers would have rather prioritized other major players than a newcomer. Therefore, a decision was taken to have EPC contracts for the three largest deliveries: topside, jacket, and SURF (subsea umbilicals, risers and flowlines). In addition, there were verification contracts and support contracts.

The goal to start production before the end of 2016 (first oil) together with the uncertainty due to the market situation was a contributing factor to the launch of the tender processes before the plan for development and operation (PDO) was approved by the authorities, despite the scepticism of the Ivar Aasen partners. However, the strategy seemed safer in light of the market situation and was probably necessary to keep to the schedule for delivering 'first oil':

> I have little doubt that if we had spent longer, we would have had a better result. However, if we had spent more time looking at the contracts, we might not have been able to secure them because all of the books would have been filled.

For some deliveries, such as transport and installation (T&I), it was critical to award the contract as early as possible in order to reserve the necessary equipment for the transport and installation of both the jacket and topside in the right time window.

Organizational complexity
The development of Ivar Aasen included a production, drilling and quarters (PDQ) platform with a steel jacket and a separate jack-up rig for drilling and completion. Today, the platform has additional slots for potential additional wells. The platform is also equipped for tie-in of a subsea template planned for possible

development of other nearby discoveries. The contracts for the development of the field are spread all over the world, from Stord in Norway to Singapore.

In order to be implemented, the project needed just over 140 different suppliers and subcontractors from different parts of the world. The project also had to relate constantly to demands (partly contradictory) from external and internal stakeholders, subproject managers, operational preparation, the Edvard Grieg field, the partnership, and the main owner of Aker BP, in addition to requirements and guidelines from the authorities.

Based on the findings, the underlying context of the Ivar Aasen project can be summarized as follows:

- The project had significant commercial importance for Det norske, since Det norske was dependent on the success of the project.
- The project was a comprehensive and organizationally complex project with respect to its size and to its diverse suppliers and subcontractors. In addition, the project had to deal with difficult relationships with the Edvard Grieg field and not least with other partners.
- There was a considerable uncertainty regarding the market situation and access to suppliers, as well as the recruitment of human resources to the project.
- The project was implemented under many strict constraints (date for first oil and strict requirements from the Edvard Grieg field), operating requirements, and various operational and functional requirements from the subprojects. Additionally, there were requirements from the authorities.
- The project organization was built simultaneously as the project evolved. There was a lack of a single team (a 'one team') from the start and some degree of lack of clarity about the internal organizational structure. Therefore, a considerable number of changes were needed to create an integrated team and to ensure an appropriate organizational structure with clear roles and responsibilities.

6.7 Learning from failure

Theoretically, through good risk and opportunity management it should be possible to identify some potential challenges and opportunities in large projects (Loosemore 2006, Hietajärvi et al. 2017), as well as to develop strategies or measures either to eliminate the sources of the challenges before they arise or to deal with the challenges and their consequences when they are encountered (Perminova et al. 2008, van Wyk et al. 2008, Zwikael and Ahn 2011). In this subchapter I provide an overview of the events and situations that caused concern or unrest in the Ivar Aasen project. I also discuss the root causes of the challenges.

The findings from the longitudinal study suggested that the Ivar Aasen project team succeeded in responding to the challenges when they arose and they succeeded in using good processes to prevent potential problems for some of the deliveries in the project. Additionally, risk management processes were used as a tool to predict potential problems or to be ready if problems arose. However, since the Ivar Aasen project was carried out under considerable pressure due to the market situation and had a complex organizational structure, it would have been better served if certain issues had been more in focus, as listed in Table 7.

Table 7 Summary of the main challenges

Issues	Suggested root causes
Internal challenges in the project organization	Lack of compatibility between the different subprojects' information systems/Fresh organization/Time pressure
External challenges with suppliers, subcontractors and the Edvard Grieg field	Insufficient FEED, lack of experience with EPC contracts and selection of suppliers, lack of dedication and buy-in, lack of a one team

The issues shown in Table 7 are complex and interrelated. For example, challenges that arose with some suppliers required closer follow-up from the project team and in some cases Det norske itself had to do the job. For example, Det norske had to mobilize over 100 people in Singapore in order to follow up the construction of the topside. In addition, Det norske had to coordinate the procurement and purchasing of package deliveries to the topside, which put even more pressure on the project organization. Delays that occurred in the topside led to weakened information flow between the subprojects. Many of the subprojects were dependent on information from the topside subproject, but they had to be kept on hold due to delays in the topside, which in turn created frustration in other subprojects.

External challenges

The study findings suggested that a number of problems in the Ivar Aasen project required a lot of resources and resulted in significant delays and cost overruns in some subprojects or to additional use of resources. The challenges encountered with the Edvard Grieg field could be attributed to both cultural and existential reasons. The Edvard Grieg project was as significant to the operator of the Edvard Grieg field (Lundin) as the Ivar Aasen project was to Det norske. The operators either wanted to succeed or had to succeed. Lundin had to complete its Edvard Grieg field in the summer and autumn of 2015. Understandably, Lundin was very protective of its field, made many demands, and had concerns about all parts that the Ivar Aasen project was intended to perform:

> Tie-in with the Edvard Grieg field was never a technically difficult challenge, but a historically notorious and culturally difficult case that could only be solved with dialogue and communication.

The interviewees were clearly of the opinion that the choice of engineering contractor was the source of problems that arose in the project. Another problem they reported was that despite the fact that the Ivar Aasen project only had agreements with a few suppliers, it appeared that the job was carried out by many different subcontractors, over which the topside contractor lacked full overview or control. The use of fines in the contracts did not prove an effective means to ensure that the best human resources were used. Also, the fixed price contract format led to commercial challenges with living quarters contractor and resulted in a large number of change orders (variation orders, VORs). The findings suggested that contractor handled its purchasing packages in an improper way and incurred extra procurement costs for Det norske.

Internal challenges

The Ivar Aasen project was a comprehensive and organizationally complex project. In addition to drilling and well operations, petroleum technology, and operational preparations, the project consisted of six main deliveries (subprojects) that were interdependent. For example, hook-up was dependent on information from the topside, as were jacket, SURF, and the living quarters. The study findings indicated that internal communication between the different subprojects was not optimal, partly due to delays in the topside, partly due to the lack of a cohesive team, and partly due to the lack of compatibility between the various information systems used by the suppliers.

Undoubtedly, the lack of human resources at the start gave the organization an opportunity to recruit qualified and competent staff for the project. It also took time to decide upon an organizational model that was clear and precise in terms of the responsibilities and relationships between the subprojects, project management, and project owners. The lack of clarity in the organization's model created confusion among the project team:

> If you have an organization chart that you have to explain for half an hour to understand how it works, then I think there's something wrong.

Additionally, the findings indicated that the quality of the FEED work was not good enough and that there were a lot of challenges and delays when it had to be transferred to the engineering contractor. In total, the engineering work was delayed by six months.

The combination of time pressure, inadequate FEED work, immature engineering organization, and the fact that the project organization was in an establishment phase created unrest in the project. This in turn spread throughout the project during the construction of the topside. During the interviews, it emerged that the situation also led to a tense atmosphere in the topside.

Furthermore, the delays complicated the flow of information between subprojects that were dependent on information from the topside.

Further, the situation resulted in stricter follow-up from the CEO:

> I sometimes felt that CEO was sitting on my shoulder.

Attempts were made to overlap engineering, construction, and procurement, yet they risky considering that the FEED work for the topside that formed the basis of the project was insufficient. The findings suggested that the project managers of the Ivar Aasen project probably underestimated the complexity of communication and interface, in both organizational and technical terms. Valuable time was lost before all the subprojects managed to cooperate:

> It took time and energy to get subprojects running in parallel.

6.8 The root causes of challenges encountered
Front-End Engineering Design (FEED) of the topside

The contract for the topside was the most comprehensive contract in the Ivar Aasen project. The topside weighed 13,700 tonnes and comprised multiple parts, such as installations for processing, gas compression, separation, water injection, flame towers, and measuring equipment. The findings suggested that there was a decision to carry out less extensive FEED work for the topside. The FEED work satisfied only the minimum requirements and was thus insufficient:

> If we wish to be diplomatic, the quality of the FEED was good enough.

The intention was to complete the design base for the topside during the engineering phase. This decision was unfortunate, since it was based on overoptimistic assumptions that proved to be challenging for the project. The assumptions were as follows:

- Continuity would be ensured by the fact that EPC contract for the topside would be awarded to the same contractor as was also responsible for the FEED. Hence, it should be easy to transfer the FEED to engineering design contractor and everything would be kept in house.
- There would not be any significant delays during the start-up of the engineering work.

Neither of the assumptions proved correct. Rather, the EPC contract was awarded to another contractor and it proved difficult to transfer the FEED to engineering. Revisions and corrections to the FEED, as well as changes to the design cost the Ivar Aasen project many additional hours (*one million extra hours*) spent on engineering, which made the work significantly more expensive than budgeted. Additionally, engineering had to be kept on hold for several months due to disagreement between the Ivar Aasen partnership and the main owner of Det norske regarding the choice of contractor for the topside. Although much work was done during the intervening period, there was little progress in the project. The work was delayed by at least six months in the first year, which put considerable pressure on the rest of the project.

Relationship with contractors and subcontractors

The interviewees reported that the working relationship with some contractors was difficult and demanding for various reasons. For instance, the engineering contractor did not have a complete organization to take care of the project. Rather, consultants were recruited as the engineering progressed. The findings suggested that the use of inexperienced consultants and lack of dedication were some of the reasons behind a number of problems that required a lot of resources and resulted in significant delays in the engineering work. The findings also showed that initial evaluation of the contractors prior contracts awarding was based on what they *promised to do* without having to present hard evidence that they were able to live up to their claims:

> We got something different from what we had been offered.

There were more than 140 purchase orders in the project and some of the subcontractors outsourced their tasks to other subcontractors without approval from Det norske. This in turn complicated follow-up, and more resources were needed in order to coordinate the purchase orders:

> Everything appeared fine at the sales stage, but when one started to follow up, one saw that there were a lot of subcontractors that they did not have control over. That was an image that became more and more clear, eventually.

The project management of the Ivar Aasen project probably did not communicate sufficiently clearly to all suppliers how important the project was for the project owner. The findings showed that the Ivar Aasen project had suppliers who did not understand the importance of the project for Det norske. Rather, they were only concerned with delivering a product and lacked dedication to the project:

> They had no sense of where they were, who they were, what they were for, etc.

Review of the measures that were used to respond to challenges with the suppliers revealed that there was less concentration on addressing the causes of the challenges than there should have been. The mobilization of human resources to cope with challenges with the suppliers was on a huge scale:

> But it was like there were bucket loads of people, pouring in more people and getting it done.

Nevertheless, the findings showed that most of the challenges with the suppliers had a *soft character*, due to lack of dedication or lack of understanding of the importance of their contribution to the project. The contractors' dedication to the project could have helped to eliminate problems related to prioritization and choice of resources:

> We have learned that it is vital to seek to understand where the other party comes from and what drives them. Usually, we are too busy telling them 'we are right'.

Inadequate information flow between subprojects

The combination of time pressure, inadequate FEED work, delays in recruiting human resources in the engineering organization, and poor information flow from engineering to construction created turbulence early in the topside. The work on the topside was behind schedule due to delays in engineering. In addition, construction work was initiated prematurely, which led to the engineering being placed under even more pressure. The project struggled with getting the various professional teams to work together in the organization:

> At one point, there were relatively many people involved and unrest, and for some time people were unsure whether this was going to succeed.

The unrest appeared to have spread further within the project during the construction of the topside. During the interviews it emerged that this situation also led to a tense atmosphere during construction of the topside. Additionally, the situation complicated the flow of information between subprojects, which were dependent on information from the topside:

> You'll get it a little later, you'll get a little later. It was a bit like 'It's not so critical now, because we're not going to have it now.' Several times, I actually hit the wall.

The findings suggested that the Ivar Aasen project probably underestimated the complexity of the interface between the subprojects in both organizational and technical terms. Valuable time was lost before all of the subprojects managed to cooperate.

Clearly, there are enormous opportunities for improvement and learning, especially with regard to investigating and assessing compatibilities between different information and computer systems at the suppliers, as a measure to uncover problems related to the interface between the subprojects. Adequate flow of information within the project organization requires closer collaboration between project teams. In the Ivar Aasen project, many measures were taken to create cohesion between subproject management:

> We went to gatherings and met regularly. We took everyone, petroleum technology, drilling and well operations. Everyone was able to join the gatherings that we held.

However, the interviewees suggest that a cohesive team for the entire Ivar Aasen project (i.e. a 'one team') was not properly in place until 2015. One interviewee described his first meeting with the Ivar Aasen team as follows:

> I came into a team in a wing where it was quiet, completely quiet. Everyone sat in complete silence and worked. So, I sat there maybe a day or two and thought: 'What is this? Is it a bank? Is it a county municipality? Isn't this a wonderful thing? Isn't this a field to be expanded? Isn't this unique? Where is the happiness and the sound of the team, and all that is going to happen?'

The interviewees reported that the lack of a 'one team' for the entire project led to the creation of subcultures in the project, each with their own culture, own slogans and own design, which weakened the whole project and impaired understanding of the dependencies (i.e. relationships) between the members. However, the interviewees emphasized that in each subproject they had gained confidence and opportunities to develop their integrated teams:

> […] those of us who have acted as subproject managers have been allowed to develop our teams completely unaffected. Complete trust and allowed to set ourselves up for success.

An important lesson that is worth drawing attention to on the basis of the interviews is that the project would have been better served by having more transparency within the management team with regards to the various challenges that the Ivar Aasen project faced. The lack of full transparency within the team was unfortunate, and the interviewees felt that lack of openness had contributed to the fact that the Ivar Aasen project did not have a 'one team' in place until 2015:

> We actually had to work to remove the fear about stating the facts, the fear of being open and sharing with their team what was going on.

The management in Ivar Aasen was cautious about informing about the delays that had occurred in 2014, in order to avoid spreading panic both up and down in the ranks. However, the interviewees believed this had the opposite effect:

> There were no smart, outgoing people who wanted to be in a position so that one could feel, see and hear what one was not getting to know about things that happened. This was incredibly important in the team.

6.9 Discussion of the lessons learned from challenges encountered
Better FEED
In the project literature, a number of researchers have emphasized the significance of good front-end processes (Artto et al. 2001, Williams and Samset 2010). The findings from the longitudinal study of the Ivar Aasen project revealed that an overlap between the concept optimization phase and detailed engineering led to a number of challenges. The interviewees' responses were in agreement that

mature FEED work could have reduced some of the problems that had arisen during the engineering and procurement phase of the project. Better FEED would have contributed to the following benefits:

- Less pressure on engineering
- Better basis for estimating the costs of package deliveries
- Reduction in the extent of interface problems between the subprojects
- Better foundation for contracting processes
- Less need for the use of additional human resources in Singapore.

Need for better interface management between subprojects

Interface management is a communications-intensive task that requires adequate and timely flow of information between subprojects and other actors in all project phases (Al-Hammad 2000, Pavitt and Gibb 2003, Nooteboom 2004, Chua and Godinot 2006, Shokri 2012). The need for a good interface is proportional to the organizational complexity of the project. The requirements for an interface between subprojects are all the more important when the project is under pressure, when attempts are made to overlap engineering, construction, and procurement, and when the FEED work that formed the basis was insufficient.

It has been claimed that good interface management is an effective tool for reducing any challenges that occur, such as those relating to information flow, requirements management, design problems, installation problems, and conflicts with suppliers (Shokri 2012). One factor that complicated interface management between the subprojects in the Ivar Aasen project was that the subprojects were run in parallel and in different parts of the world, thus creating significant communication and interface challenges. Additionally, contracts for the subprojects were placed before the scope of work had been adequately defined. Problems related to interface management have been reported as one of the main causes of cost overruns in oil and gas projects (Nooteboom 2004).

Chua and Godinot (2006) distinguish between four categories of interface management: organizational, technical, geographical, and time. The findings from the Ivar Aasen project confirmed that all four interface categories were challenged in the project (Table 8).

Table 8 Interface management problems between the subprojects

Challenge	Interface management category
Complications in the transfer of information from the topside contractor to hook-up	Organizational
Interface management was not optimal, partly due to delays in the topside	Time and geographical
Insufficient interface with the Edvard Grieg field	Organizational and technical
Challenging interface between living quarters and the topside	Technical and geographical
Tense relationship with the operator of the Edvard Grieg field	Organizational and technical
Change of functional requirements without approval	Technical
Inadequate involvement of operations	Organizational and geographical
Information flow between engineering and package deliveries	Organizational

Problems with the Edvard Grieg field can be linked to both *cultural* and existential causes. In general, external relationships can be improved through good processes for understanding the landscape of stakeholders in the project (Aaltonen and Kujala 2016). In this regard, there appears to be opportunities for improvement and learning, especially when it comes to developing response strategies for managing key stakeholders who place demands or who are not necessarily cooperative (Aaltonen and Sivonen 2009).

Furthermore, it is clear that there are enormous opportunities for improvement and learning, especially with regard to investigating and assessing information systems compatibility between the suppliers' different information and data systems, as a means to uncover problems related to the interface between the subprojects.

Need for building a 'one team' from the first day

Many measures were taken in the Ivar Aasen project to build cohesion and relations between subproject leaders, but the cohesive team (a 'one team') was not properly in place until 2015. Building a cohesive team is a difficult task, due to various personal, bureaucratic and organizational barriers (Song and Parry 1997). One of the most important factors that can help to build a cohesive team is to create among the team members both solidarity and understanding of the interdependency between their respective tasks (Pinto 2012). This is a demanding process and should therefore be initiated as early as possible in the project. In the Ivar Aasen project, the experiences from drilling and well operations and the petroleum technology confirmed that good communications, understanding of the organic dependency relationships, and cohesion between them contributed to substantial cost savings. The concept of a 'one team' is not only about using practical or visual measures to emphasize the interdependency between the subprojects, but also involves nurturing and creating loyalty to the decisions taken in the team. Any changes beyond what has been decided should require discussion and new decisions.

Need to focus on suppliers' dedication

Some of the sources of a number of problems that required a lot of resources and resulted in significant delays and cost overruns were lack of maturity, lack of experience, the use of inexperienced consultants, inadequate tendering, and hasty contracting. The interviewees emphasized that the most important lesson learned was not only to ensure that the suppliers had the required engineering and project management tools, but also that they were able to *demonstrate the ability, competence, and willingness* to use them. Additionally, the evaluation of the suppliers should be based on their ability to use different project tools.

A review of the measures used to respond to the challenges faced in terms of the suppliers revealed that insufficient attention had been paid to addressing the real causes of the lack of dedication from some of the suppliers.

The findings also showed that most of the challenges relating to the suppliers were soft in character. Having good contracting processes is important, but it is equally important to place great emphasis on a good working relationship between the project and the contractors, one that is based on trust, openness and transparency (Milosevic 1990, Das and Bing-Sheng 1998, Zaghloul and Hartman 2003, Kadefors 2004, Pinto et al. 2009, Lau and Rowlinson 2011).

Trust between the supplier and the project owner is a complex matter. Although the meaning of the 'trust' may change over time, it is currently defined as the willingness to accept risks. Trust has a great influence in decision-making because decisions are made on the basis of both trust and the understanding of the risks involved. Good cooperation between the contractor and suppliers is more dependent on mutual trust than, for example, on formal agreements. The project must communicate this trust to the supplier.

In the Ivar Aasen project, the need to communicate trust to the supplier was well demonstrated in the case of the delivery of the jacket. The subproject managed to create a good working relationship with the contractor Saipem. The working environment was established through both parties having a shared sense of where they were heading and knowing how to solve problems when there were disagreements. Their way of thinking was achieved through good preparation and was established during contract negotiations.

Experiences from the drilling and well operations showed the importance of communicating to the suppliers that the project needed their expertise. Such needs should be communicated openly and clearly to the supplier.

The supplier should have an opportunity to influence and be an active participant in the project instead of waiting for instructions or for orders to arrive. This is necessary in order to create a real sense of ownership of the project and to reduce the need for control and management:

> Because we have demanded that they should challenge us too, we are not going to just sit and make orders. So, this has been another way of working.

There is probably a need for new forms of collaborations that would allow for better integration between the involved parties (Errasti et al. 2007, Smyth and Edkins 2007, Yeung et al. 2007, Børve et al. 2017) or to establish networks of alliances between suppliers and the project owner (Hietajärvi et al. 2017). In other words, suppliers should be an integral part of the project organization and should be given the encouragement and opportunity to make their own recommendations for how the tasks should best be performed.

Alliancing is a broad concept the emphasizes interorganizational cooperation and collaboration (Chen et al. 2012). The term 'alliancing' is used to describe various types of collaborative ventures, ranging from longer term strategic business relationships to short-term arrangements whereby owners and service providers come together to deliver a single project, with all kinds of applications between the two extremes (Rowlinson et al. 2006). The most commonly adopted definition of strategic alliances is the establishment of interorganizational relations and engagement in collaborative behaviour for a specific purpose (Love and Gunasekaran 1999), whereas project alliances are described as project delivery strategies (Hutchinson and Gallagher 2003). A project alliance focuses on developing an integrated high-performance team. Project alliances is based on three principles: (1) risks and gain sharing, (2) no fault, no blame and no dispute, and (3) commitments to trust, collaboration, innovation, and mutual support (Hutchinson and Gallagher 2003). In comparison, strategic alliancing is a governance structure established for a specific purpose or in order to collaborate on a series of projects or programmes (Hoffmann and Schlosser 2001). An overview of studies of factors that influence alliance success is provided by Kogut (1988).

Need for transparency

The initial phase of the Ivar Aasen project was demanding, which in turn influenced the collaboration between progress, H&S, and information flow between the subprojects. The situation also resulted in stricter follow-up from the director and may be perceived as distrust on the part of the project participants. An important insight gained from the interviews is that the project would have been better served by having more transparency within the management team with regard to the various challenges that the project faced.

Transparency is a virtue that involves openness and availability or disclosure of information. Within the field of organizational behaviour, transparency may be conceptualized at the organizational level as informational justice, which entails providing explanations about organizational procedures and being thorough, candid, timely, and considerate toward others' specific needs in communications about those procedures. At the project level or team level, transparency means the sharing of relevant information and explanations within a team, and has been suggested as a moderating factor to increase a team's ability to adhere to its commitments to organizational tasks (Palanski et al. 2011).

6.10 Learning from success

There were a number of challenges along the way in the Ivar Aasen project, right up until the final day. The challenges were handled and addressed in different ways and by using different approaches, by different teams:

> I've been working here for six years. Not everything has been a bed of roses, but I've never had a boring day.

This subchapter summarizes the most important measures that were used to ensure completion of the project.

A good working environment based on trust and backing

In the Ivar Aasen project, the dedication of the project team was a critical factor in addressing many of the challenges posed by suppliers and interface. The study findings indicated that those involved the project were willing to go the extra mile. It was also clear that the project teams were given the opportunity to use their expertise and initiative without having to go through long decision-making processes. Additionally, good processes were used to create a sense of ownership among the project team members. Thus, the project team's dedication and efforts were crucial for the project's success, despite the challenges that arose.

Furthermore, the interviewees indicated that there was mutual trust between project leadership and project managers of the subprojects. The interviewees also described the power structure in the organization as flat, which might have contributed to the high level of trust in the organization (Smyth et al. 2010).

Nijhof et al. (1998) and McLeod and MacDonell (2011) are all in agreement that dedication of senior management and the project organization is an important success factor in projects.

Quick mobilization

An important contribution to the success of the Ivar Aasen project was that the challenges were addressed as soon as they arose. Most of the challenges were handled through a hands-on approach, with good ability to adjust and quick mobilization of human resources to troubled subprojects. In a project such as the Ivar Aasen project, in which one does not have the opportunity to predict all possible challenges, it is important to put in place appropriate measure when the problems arise:

> Aker BP always expressed their cooperation as being not only 'hands on', but additionally 'hands in'.

The communication between the project team members and project management or the senior management was informal and provided good flexibility to deal with challenges. In such contexts, decision-making requires *critical and analytical judgment* and is based on facts and accumulated knowledge (Rolstadås et al. 2014). This applies even when project managers are presented with incomplete and ambiguous information. Müller and Turner (2010) show that successful project managers have a strong need for competence in critical and analytical judgment.

Clear priorities

An important consequence of the tie-in solution with the Edvard Grieg field was that it gave the Ivar Aasen project an opportunity to have the first oil in the fourth quarter of 2016, the target stuck to by the project management. The study findings indicated that it was a wise decision to keep to that date, despite the problems and challenges that arose along the way. By locking the project to an end date, the project organization had set a goal that helped the project to be dedicated and to create an efficient, integrated team:

> We said that we had a goal and it was delivery in the fourth quarter of 2016, and then it was important that one had faith in the goal.

Due to delays in the engineering work, many considered it necessary to allow engineering more time. However, the project management kept its decision and thought it was too early to use the time reserve, and many were encouraged by this thinking and supported the decision.

In retrospect, it can be concluded that the decision to keep the end date might have been the main reason why the project managed to create the necessary driving force to reverse a negative trend. Locking the project end date also served as an important signal, led to robustness in the organization, and reassured stakeholders who lacked faith in its ability to deliver:

> I just had to send that signal. I assumed that we were to deliver this project, and therefore I used the word 'guarantee'.

Clear communication of the project management's expectations of project team members is essential as a source of *inspiration and stimulation*. According to

Anantatmula (2010), clear communication of priorities and expectations is important in order to encourage team member to manage their tasks within the framework of the overall objectives of the project from the first day, and thus create a driving force for improvement.

The determination to succeed

As the first project for the Norwegian operator Det norske, the Ivar Aasen project had great commercial significance for the company. In turn, the project was dependent on the success of Det norske and the mutual dependency created determination and commitment in all aspects of the organization and was therefore a driving force for success in the project:

> We sought to succeed.

Several interviewees reported that there was strong and affectionate commitment to succeed, which is considered critical to project success (Leung et al. 2004). The affectionate commitment to project success was strengthened by the understanding and acknowledgement of the impact of the project on the entire organization.

Autonomy

The study findings indicated that human resources in the Ivar Aasen project were given the opportunity to use their skills and initiative, without having to resort to complex decision-making processes in order to obtain prior approval. For instance, the interviewees argued that, to some extent, they had gained autonomy at both project level and subproject level, which reinforced their dedication to the project:

> […] those of us who have acted as subproject managers have been allowed to develop our teams completely unaffected. Complete trust and allowed to set ourselves up for success.

Autonomy is a sense of freedom and independence in one's work. It is an important factor in creating what organizational theorists call intellectual stimulation

(Bass and Riggio 2006). Autonomy is also important for maintaining internal motivation, dedication and more learning (Jønsson and Jeppesen 2013). The high degree of autonomy in the Ivar Aasen project was important for responding to the various challenges and for giving the subprojects the chance to take advantage of the opportunities that arose along the way.

Visible and supportive project leadership

The interviewees emphasized that autonomy was combined with close follow-up by the project management. The project management was able to be visible and effective whenever necessary. They gave clear feedback but remained sufficiently in the background and gave more autonomy to the subproject managers. According to Foss and Christensen (2011), balancing autonomy with feedback, follow-up and visibility can reduce the risk of project team members developing an egoistic approach to their work, whereby they do what they themselves think is interesting and do not conform to overall guidelines and expectations. Too much autonomy can also cause unfortunate consequences if project members experience it as a lack of management (Langfred 2004). Oldham and Hackman (2010) claim that giving feedback to project participants is important not only for motivation but also for personal development.

Dedicated project owner

An important factor that contributed to the success of the project was the senior management in Det norske. A visible, and clear leadership was especially important in order to deal with difficult negotiations with external stakeholders. It was also especially important for those who were internal project owners. It was clear that the internal project owners had sufficient authority to concentrate attention on the most important parts of the project that were necessary for success, which from the external owner's perspective was to produce oil and ensure that the project had a good economy.

The need for an owner who communicates clearly and is good at decision-making is all the more important when there are diverse decision-making bases. In a project such as the Ivar Aasen project, in which everything happened at the same time, there is no time available in which to document a comprehensive basis for decision-making.

Turning points

Many interviewees described 2013 and 2014 as difficult years that were characterized by unrest. In any organization, the turning points in a project will provide a boost. There will be hope of reaching the goal when the project is on the right course, and this will have a significant psychological effect on the project participants. Turning points mark a transition from just believing in success to demonstrating the ability to achieve success. The interviewees indicated that the Ivar Aasen project had two key turning points that changed the psychological context of the entire project. The first turning point was the start of Maersk Interceptor, which proved to be the first subproject that was successful:

> But the wonderful Maersk Interceptor, which came out to the field and just got on drilling and behaved like the devil and delivered so that it stayed at the top of the world.

The contract with Maersk stated that the rig could begin between December 2014 and March 2015. The project assumed that the rig would come late in this window, but the assumption was rejected by the leaders of the drilling and well operations:

> We have a contract with Maersk, which states that the rig can come in December, that is, half a year early. So, we have to make a plan that takes this into account. If not ... to sit with a rig for half a year without using it will be a reasonably hefty cost.

Drilling and well operations prepared a plan for the use of the rig if it arrived early. Petroleum technology was also interested to participate in the plan prepared by drilling and well operations. The Ivar Aasen field had not been very well mapped and one of the reasons was found in the neighbouring license, a discovery that was unitized with the Ivar Aasen field. Petroleum technology had a strong desire to drill pilot wells, both in order to learn more and to optimize the location of production and injection wells.

The rig was not delayed and was available for the project from 28 December 2014, thus giving drilling and well operations and petroleum technology six months in which to drill before the jacket was in place. Five pilot wells were drilled, which enabled the project to become familiar with the rig before the drilling of production wells started. This in turn made both drilling and well operations and petroleum technology even more effective. The second turning point was when the jacket was put in place in the summer of 2015, which was within the project's time frame.

7 Contingent classification of the lessons learned

I have shown that abstraction from single occurrences and events in order to formulate more general recommendations is a repeated challenge in cognitive practices. What is learned within a project might be of a little value for other projects, due to the customized and specific nature of each project. The approach adopted in the longitudinal study of the Ivar Aasen project in order to develop relevant lessons learned for future projects was to associate the collected lessons learned to the underlying characteristics of the project. In the next section, I present the results of associating with project characteristics with both the identified lessons learned on drivers of success and the lessons learned on the root causes of challenges. Some important characteristic identified in the Ivar Aasen project are as follows:

- The project had significant commercial importance for Det norske, since Det norske was dependent on the success of the project.
- The project was a comprehensive and organizationally complex project with respect to its size and to its diverse suppliers and subcontractors. In addition, the project had to deal with difficult relationships with the Edvard Grieg field and not least with other partners. In addition, the project organization in the project was built simultaneously as the project evolved. There was lack of a single team (a 'one team') from the start and some degree of lack of clarity about the internal organizational structure. Therefore, a considerable number of changes were needed to create an integrated team and to ensure an appropriate organizational structure with clear roles and responsibilities.
- There was a considerable uncertainty regarding the market situation and access to suppliers, as well as the recruitment of human resources to the

project. The project was implemented under many strict constraints (the date for first oil and strict requirements from the Edvard Grieg field), operating requirements, and various operational and functional requirements from the subprojects. Additionally, there were requirements from the authorities.

Based on the findings presented in Chapter 6, the most important characteristics of the Ivar Aasen project and the associated lessons learned are summarized in the following sections.

Organizationally complex project

The project included several subdeliveries with mutual dependencies. The coordination of design, construction, procurement, and installation of all subdeliveries is a technical and structurally complex task. In the case of the Ivar Aasen project, the sources of the challenges were not only the size and/or scale of the work involved, but also the diversity in the project's internal and external stakeholders. In order to be implemented, the project needed just over 140 different suppliers and subcontractors from different parts of the world. The project also had to relate constantly to demands (partly contradictory) from external and internal stakeholders, subproject managers, operational preparation, the Edvard Grieg field, the partnership, and the main owner of Aker BP, in addition to requirements and guidelines from the authorities. The study findings confirmed that in order to succeed in such a complex task in the best possible way, the following lessons learned should be adopted:

- The project has to create good arenas and processes to maintain an efficient flow of information between all subdeliveries in all phases in which the suppliers are involved.
- The quality of the end product depends on the competence and dedication of those who perform and coordinate all of the tasks. Therefore, the project management must ensure that all subprojects, suppliers and subcontractors are staffed with human resources with have sufficient expertise and experience in all aspects.
- Suppliers must have compatible information systems for the transmission and sharing of important data during different project phases.

- In order to succeed in the interface between subdeliveries, the suppliers must *demonstrate their ability and expertise* to utilize their project management tools and information systems in all project phases.
- Within the project organization, complexity requires a solid understanding of dependency relations and solidarity between all subprojects (a 'one team') in order to reduce any communication problems. Therefore, processes and measures should be initiated as early as possible to create a sense of 'one team' with the suppliers.
- Good stakeholder analysis should be performed and good strategies should be developed for managing different stakeholder categories as early as possible in the project. Additionally, extra effort should be put into developing strategies for managing stakeholders who have a great influence but who are not necessarily supportive of the project.
- Relationships between suppliers and subcontractors must be based on trust and cooperation, not just on formal agreements. The suppliers must understand their importance to the project and understand the mutual dependency between themselves and the project owners.
- The suppliers should have an opportunity to influence and be active participants in the project, rather than sitting and waiting for instructions or for orders to arrive. This is necessary in order to create real sense of ownership of the project and to reduce the need for control and management.
- There is probably a need for new forms of contracts that would allow for more cooperation between suppliers and project owners. This would mean that suppliers would be an integral part of the project organization, with the opportunity to make their own recommendations for how the tasks should best be performed.
- It is important for the project organization to have the ability to change and learn from its errors along the way.

The Ivar Aasen project had significant commercial impact

It is crystal clear that the Ivar Aasen project was more than just a project for Det norske: the fate of Det norske was dependent on the success of the Ivar Aasen project and vice versa, which created a unique situation. The project literature highlights that such unique situations are prerequisites for organizational success. The unique situation in the Ivar Aasen project created an organic dependency between the business goals of Det norske and the Ivar Aasen project's target. It is not an exaggeration to state that the organizational culture of Det norske was coloured by the project culture in the Ivar Aasen project. The study findings revealed that it is necessary to ensure that the following factors are in place when the project has a major impact on the organization:

- Competent, visible and clear leadership in the role of internal project owners, who should be capable of following up and addressing challenges as soon as they arise.
- The project owner should have sufficient authority to mobilize and provide support, as well as to pay attention, to the most important parts of the project that are necessary for success.
- Maintenance and strengthening of awareness of the impact of the project on the entire organization.

The Ivar Aasen project was carried out under time pressure and market uncertainty

The time pressure in the Ivar Aasen project was highly visible and influenced the many of the decisions taken. The intention was clear: to start production (i.e. 'first oil') in the fourth quarter of 2016. Keeping to the schedule in a difficult market situation is difficult for a project such as the Ivar Aasen project. Few main suppliers had any wish to work for a small newcomer such as Det norske, and Det norske could not choose suppliers from the top shelf. This in turn contributed to a number of the decisions taken, including the following:

- The bidding processes was started before the FEED work had been completed. For some deliveries such as transport and installation (T&I), it was critical to award the contract as early as possible in order to preserve the necessary equipment in the right time window.
- Attempts were made to overlap engineering with the construction of the topside, which put more pressure on engineering.

The above findings show that the following conditions are necessary when the project is to be carried out in a tight time window and in a situation with market pressure:

- Overlapping between engineering, construction or procurement activities during the project should be considered only if the design basis of the project is adequate.
- Introduce measures and processes to prevent the challenges that occur in one phase spreading to the next phase. Being open about challenges that arise in one phase can enhance individuals' and team members' motivation and sense of responsibility, and reduce the risk of unrest in subsequent phases.
- Project plans should be based to a lesser extent on optimistic assumptions about project development, continuity, awarding contracts, and the ability of the suppliers. For example, it was assumed that SMOE, which had just completed an EPC project for Conoco Philips, would be able to handle an EPC contract for the Ivar Aasen project, but this proved not to be the case. It was also assumed that continuity would be ensured by the fact that engineering would be awarded to Aker Solutions, which was also responsible for the FEED, and therefore it should be easy to transfer the FEED to engineering. This, too, proved to be incorrect.
- Keep to the schedule and use it as a tool to create a sense of unity and a driving force. Keeping to the end date might have been the main reason why the Ivar Aasen project managed to create the necessary driving force to reverse a negative trend.
- It is especially important to communicate the project's frameworks, roles, responsibilities, expectations, and priorities to all stakeholders, and to encourage team members at both project level and subproject level to manage their tasks within those limits.
- Project managers should be good at giving clear feedback and should be visible but should also provide autonomy to individuals and subproject managers. Balancing autonomy with feedback, follow-up and visibility can reduce the risk of project team members doing what they themselves think is interesting rather than conforming to the overall goals of the project. However, too much autonomy can have unfortunate consequences because teams will experience it as lack of management. Autonomy is also necessary in order to be able to respond quickly to different challenges or to exploit any opportunities that arise. The use of Maersk Interceptor and the results subsequently achieved serves as a good example of the consequences of giving project projects teams a considerable degree of autonomy.

- Introduce good routines for change control. The management of the Ivar Aasen project was aware of this condition and had a no-change policy in order to regulate changes and adjustments along the way.
- Create a culture in which project team members are encouraged to improve their tasks continually.
- Work more consciously towards such turning points in the project and subprojects in order to create self-esteem and driving force for project participants so that they will shift their perspective from just believing in success to realizing achieving success is possible.

8 Did we really learn the lessons?

Thus far in this book, the chapters have provided a wealth of lessons learned from the Ivar Aasen project. Additionally, readers should have gained an understanding of the relationship or association between these lessons learned and the project context. I should also mention that in a large-scale project such as the Ivar Aasen project, it is neither possible nor feasible to identify all the lessons learned or to describe with accuracy all the past events or details of those events that took place during the conception, planning and execution. The identified lessons learned have been presented to the management of the Ivar Aasen and to several project participants, and they have acknowledged that the narratives provided in this book provide an accurate picture regarding the main events in the project. In this chapter, I attempt to close the loop of learning by answering the following research question:

Did Aker BP learn the lessons from the Ivar Aasen project?

The research carried out to answer the question was done out two years after project completion. If the achievement of learning or the impact of learning had been measured immediately after completion, the results would not have been sufficiently accurate or credible for reflection or for gaining deep insights into what constitute good methods to evaluate learning impact.

Method

In order to answer the research question, I devised a questionnaire that consisted of a combination of open questions, questions with multiple answers, and questions with Likert-scale responses. The questionnaire was sent by e-mail to project team members who were involved in different projects. Although the number of valid responses was limited (19 valid responses), the responses provided a good overall view of the organization's ability to take advantage of the knowledge gained from Ivar Aasen project. In addition, the respondents provided some useful insights into how to improve learning efforts in the case company. The questionnaire consisted of three main parts:

- Respondents' evaluation of the relevance and usefulness of the lessons learned from Ivar Aasen to their current projects. In many respects, this set of questions was intended to measure the ability of the process outlined in Chapter 6 to identify and establish lessons learned that have relevance to future projects and/or provide additional new knowledge or that affirmed the respondent's previous knowledge.
- Respondents' evaluation of the impact of learning on their current projects.
- Respondents' evaluation of how far their organization has reused the identified lessons learned from the Ivar Aasen project, as outlined in Chapter 7.

In addition to answering the questions, the respondents were given opportunities to comment on and make suggestions for improving learning or the reuse of lessons learned.

8.1 Evaluation of the relevance and usefulness of the lessons learned

For the set of questions designed to evaluate the relevance and usefulness of the lessons learned from the Ivar Aasen project, the respondents were asked to express their opinions on Likert scale (strongly agree, agree, neutral, disagree and strongly disagree) or to answer 'D not know' to the following statements:

1. The lessons are applicable to my current projects.
2. The lessons provided me with new knowledge or reaffirmed previous knowledge.

The first question was used to assess the relevance of the defined lesson learned to current project and the second question was used to assess the usefulness of the lessons learned for the respondents' knowledge base. The responses to the questions are shown in Table 9.

Table 9 Respondents' evaluation of relevance and usefulness of the lessons learned from the Ivar Aasen project

Statement	Strongly agree	Agree	Neutral	Disagree	Strongly disagree	Do not know
The lessons are applicable to my current projects	12%	47%	18%	0%	0%	23%
The lessons provided me with new knowledge or reaffirmed previously acquired knowledge	0%	65%	12%	6 %	0%	18%

Results shown in Table 9 show that the percentage of the respondents who agreed or strongly agreed that the identified lessons from the Ivar Aasen project were applicable to their current projects was 59%, whereas none of the respondents disagreed or strongly disagreed. Similarly, the percentage of the respondents who agreed or strongly agreed that the identified lessons from Ivar Aasen contributed to new knowledge or reaffirmed the previous knowledge was 62%, while only 6% disagreed or strongly disagreed. These results are good indicators that the lessons learned from Ivar Aasen were relevant to the respondents current work assignments and their knowledge base.

8.2 Evaluation of the impact of lessons learned

In subchapter 1.2 I have presented a short literature review to outline the impact of learning or why learning matters. Through the review, I have shown that learning matters because it can contribute in the following ways:

- Provides insights into good practices and methods for correcting errors or solving problems
- Provides insights into possible underlying causes of problems in projects
- Helps to avoid repetition of the same mistakes
- Helps to refine existing ways of doing things but avoiding the risks of experimentation
- Enables insights to be gained into the drivers of success
- Increases the knowledge base and/or assets of the organization

- Improves project management competency at individual, team and organization levels
- Improves the learning culture at individual, team and organization levels.

Based on these insights and in order to evaluate the impact of learning from the Ivar Aasen project, I devised a set of postulates. The postulates cover the potential impact of learning in three clusters:

- Individual/team level. The objective was to assess the impact of learning with respect to the following: project management competency level, insights gained, conditions of success, confidence, and inspiring individuals and teams to appreciate knowledge sharing.
- Project level. The objective was to assess the impact of learning directly on some project-related parameters, including time, conflicts level and the introduction of new working methods.
- Organizational level. The objective was to assess the impact of learning on the entire organization, ranging from project management competency to culture.

Accordingly, the respondents were asked to express their support for the postulates on a Likert scale (strongly agree, agree, neutral, disagree, strongly disagree) or to answer 'Do not know'. The results are shown in Table 10.

Table 10 Postulates to assess the impact of learning

Postulates	Objective
Helped me/my team to save time	Assess the impact at the project level
Helped me/my team to avoid conflicts or misunderstandings with various stakeholders	Assess the impact at the project level
Helped me to gain valuable insights into the conditions of success in my current project	Assess the impact at the project level
My competency as a project manager/team member has increased	Assess the impact at the individual level
Project competency within my team/unit has increased	Assess the impact at the team level
Project competency within Aker BP has increased	Assess the impact at the organizational level
Has contributed to a better lessons-learned culture in Aker BP	Assess the impact at the organizational level
We are now doing projects differently because of the lessons learned from the Ivar Aasen project	Assess the impact at the project level
Has strengthened my belief that our team/my unit will succeed in our task/assignment	Assess the impact at the team/individual level
Has inspired me/my team to appreciate collaboration and knowledge sharing	Assess the impact at the team/individual level

The results of the respondents' response to each postulate, rounded to the nearest whole number, are shown in Table 11.

Table 11 The impact of the lessons learned

Statement	Strongly Agree	Agree	Neutral	Disagree	Strongly Disagree	Do not know
Helped me/my team to save time	12%	53%	12%	18%	0%	5%
Helped me/my team to avoid potential conflicts/misunderstandings with various stakeholders	18%	35%	35%	6%	0%	6%
Helped me to gain valuable insights into the conditions of success in my current project	24%	41%	30%	0%	0%	5%
My competency as a project manager/team member has increased	29%	47%	12%	6%	0%	5%
Project competency within my team/unit has increased	24%	53%	6%	12%	0%	6%
Project competency within Aker BP has increased	12%	53%	24%	6%	0%	5%
Has contributed to a better lessons-learned culture in Aker BP	6%	29%	47%	12%	0%	6%
We are now doing projects differently because of the lessons learned from the Ivar Aasen project	0%	47%	24%	6%	0%	23%
Has strengthened my belief that our team/my unit will succeed in our task/assignment	18%	47%	29%	0%	0%	6%
Has inspired me/my team to appreciate collaboration and knowledge sharing	24%	47%	24%	0%	0%	6%

In addition, one sample T-test was conducted to rank the degree of support (strongly agree or agree) for the postulates. The results of the T-test are shown in Table 12. A T-test measures variation in the measured means in the sample.

The greater the magnitude of T, the greater the evidence that the postulate has been fulfilled. By contrast, a p-value is the calculated probability that the T-value will change if the sample population (i.e. used to calculate the T-value) were changed. The closer the p-value to 0, the more unlikely it is that the T-value will be changed.

Table 12 Ranking of the impact of the lessons learned

Rank		T-value	p-value
1	Has inspired me/my team to appreciate collaboration and knowledge sharing	5.1	.000
2	My competency as a project manager/ team member has increased	4.9	.000
3	Helped me to gain valuable insights into conditions of success in my projects	4.5	.000
4	Has strengthened my belief that my team will succeed in our task/assignment	4.5	.000
5	Project competency within my team/unit has increased	3.8	.002
6	Project competency within Aker BP has increased	3.6	.003
7	We are now doing projects differently because of the lessons learned from the Ivar Aasen project	2.9	.012
8	Helped me/my team to avoid potential conflicts/ misunderstandings with various stakeholders	2.9	.012
9	Helped me/my team to save time	2.4	.033
10	Has contributed to a better lessons-learned culture in Aker BP	2.1	.054

The results of the T-test may be interpreted as indicating that the respondents expressed strong support for the following postulates regarding the contribution of the lessons learned from the Ivar Aasen project:

- Inspired individuals to appreciate collaboration and knowledge sharing
- Increased project management competency at an individual level
- Provided valuable insights into conditions of success
- Strengthened the belief in succeeding.

Furthermore, the results indicate that perceived impact of learning is of a relatively soft character, such as inspiring, gaining insights, strengthening belief, and increasing competency. These indicators are subjective in nature – we can feel them, but we cannot quantify them. The results may also suggest that the greatest impact of having structured processes for developing lessons learned is that the lessons contribute to individual attitudes that are more positive towards learning and knowledge sharing.

The results may also suggest that the respondent's expressed adequate support for the following postulates regarding the contribution of the lessons learned from the Ivar Aasen project:

- Increased project competency within the team/unit
- Increased project competency within Aker BP
- Improved project execution
- Reduction in potential conflicts/misunderstandings with various stakeholders
- Time savings.

The results particularly provide evidence of the positive impact of the lessons learned at the project level, as well as in terms of improving current practices, saving time, conflict avoidance, improved project competency at both the project level and the organizational level.

Finally, the results suggest that respondents expressed less support for the postulate that the lessons learned had contributed to a better lessons-learned culture in Aker BP.

An overall assessment of the results may suggest that the strength of the impact of the lessons learned from one project gradually decreases with the shift the individual level to project level and upwards to the organizational level.

8.3 Evaluation of the reuse of lessons learned

Further to the discussion in Chapter 7 on the reuse of lessons learned in the Ivar Aasen project, the respondents were asked to select one of four alternatives for each lesson learned:

- The lesson was applicable to my current project and was followed through.
- The lesson was applicable to my current project but was not followed through.

- The lesson was not applicable to my current project.
- I do not know/no answer.

The results of the respondent's responses are shown in Tables 13 and Table 14. Table 13 shows the list of the lessons learned that the majority of the respondents stated were applicable and either followed through or not followed through in their projects.

The results shown in Table 13 may suggest that over 80% of the lessons learned in the Ivar Aasen project had been adequately applied and followed through in the respondents' current projects. If that was the case, it would not only have been a very satisfactory achievement but might also suggest that the organization as a whole was able to take advantage of the available body of knowledge generated by the Ivar Aasen project. In particular, it appears that seven lessons learned were fully learned (i.e. applied and followed through in the respondents' current projects):

- Efforts should be made so that the contractors/suppliers understand their importance to the project.
- Relationships between the operator, suppliers and subcontractors should be based on mutual trust, not just on formal agreements.
- The suppliers should be given a real opportunity to influence the project development in a positive way.
- The project organization should have the ability to change and learn from its errors along the way.
- A culture should be created in which project team members are encouraged to improve their tasks continually.
- The project's frameworks, roles, responsibilities, expectations, and priorities should be communicated to all stakeholders.
- It is important to keep to the original schedule/deadlines and use that as a means to create a sense of unity and a driving force.

The above-listed findings strongly suggest that Aker BP had adapted and changed its collaboration approaches with its suppliers and subcontractors. This was probably due to the increasing use of alliances networks in the company. In addition, the findings strongly suggest that the culture of learning and improving

Table 13 Applicable and followed-through lessons learned from the Ivar Aasen project

Lessons learned	Support	
	Applicable and followed through	Applicable but not followed through
Efforts should be made so that the contractors/suppliers understand their importance to the project.	76.47%	5.88%
The project organization should have the ability to change and learn from its errors along the way.	76.47%	17.65%
A culture should be created in which project team members are encouraged to improve their tasks continually.	76.47%	11.76%
Relationships between the operator, suppliers and subcontractors should be based on mutual trust, not just on formal agreements.	70.59%	11.76%
The project's frameworks, roles, responsibilities, expectations, and priorities should be communicated to all stakeholders.	70.59%	23.53%
The suppliers should be given a real opportunity to influence the project development in a positive way.	64.71%	23.53%
It is important to keep to the original schedule/deadlines and use that as a means to create a sense of unity and a driving force.	64.71%	17.65%
Maintain an adequate flow of information between all subprojects/deliverables in all phases.	58.82%	23.53%
All subprojects/deliverables should be staffed with skilled and experienced people in all relevant aspects.	58.82%	23.53%
Stronger focus should be placed on front-end engineering design (FEED) processes.	52.94%	23.53%
Stronger emphasizes should be placed on being transparent about challenges and problems encountered.	52.94%	35.29%
Top management should be visible.	52.94%	35.29%
Mobilize and provide support to the most important parts of the project that are necessary for success.	52.94%	35.29%
Project plans should be based on realistic assumptions about project development, continuity, and the ability of the suppliers.	47.06%	35.29%
Autonomy should be provided at all levels.	41.18%	35.29%

performance had been maintained in the respondents' current projects. Furthermore, the findings suggest the aforementioned culture was combined with both a continuous and robust commitment to achieve target goals and a commitment to communicating priorities and expectations to project staff.

However, findings suggest that the following lessons learned from the Ivar Aasen project might need stronger emphasis placed on them by the senior management:

- Stronger emphasizes should be placed on being *transparent* about challenges and problems encountered.
- Top management should be *visible*.
- Mobilize and provide *support* to the most important parts of the project that are necessary for success.
- Project plans should be based on *realistic assumptions* about project development, continuity, and the ability of the suppliers.
- *Autonomy* should be provided at all levels.

The above-listed lessons learned appear to be issues that management of the company should take into account and find means to deal with, as they are mainly managerial tasks and require top management to be visible, give quick responses, be able to provide support to and mobilize important parts of the project, and provide more autonomy for the project teams.

Table 14 shows the list of the lessons learned that the respondents stated were relevant to their current projects but had not been followed through adequately.

The results shown in Table 14 may suggest that although some previously defined lessons learned were applicable, there was less evidence to suggest that they had been accurately applied. The lessons from Ivar Aasen that are considered applicable by the respondents but not followed through in current projects include:

- Autonomy should be balanced with feedback, follow-up and visibility
- Maintain and strengthen awareness of the impact of the project on the entire organization
- Work more consciously towards achieving intermediate results (turning points) in the project in order to create self-esteem and a driving force
- Suppliers/contractors should have compatible information systems for the sharing of important data during different project phases.

Table 14 Applicable but not followed through lessons learned from the Ivar Aasen project

Lessons learned	Support	
	Applicable and followed through	Applicable but not followed through
Autonomy should be balanced with feedback, follow-up and visibility	35.29%	47.06%
Work more consciously towards achieving intermediate results (turning points) in the project in order to create self-esteem and a driving force	35.29%	35.29%
Maintain and strengthen awareness of the impact of the project on the entire organization	35.29%	52.94%
Suppliers/contractors should have compatible information systems for the sharing of important data during different project phases	23.53%	47.06%

The issues were mainly managerial tasks that needed to be focused on more adequately, which included balancing autonomy with good follow-up and feedback, and an ability to maintain and strengthen awareness of the impact of the project on the entire organization. Additionally, project management should strengthen the project execution culture by focusing more consciously on achieving intermediate results (turning points) in the project.

8.4 Final remarks

In this subchapter I summarize the respondents' responses to three categories of questions that designed for the following purposes:

- Assess the relevance and value of learning from the Ivar Aasen project for the respondents' current projects.
- Assess the impact of learning from the Ivar Aasen project at the individual, project and organizational levels.
- Assess the reuse of lessons learned in the respondents' current projects.

The overall conclusions drawn from the analysis of the results obtained from the longitudinal study suggest that not only did the Ivar Aasen project manage to deliver its project objectives, but also that the project had a substantial impact on learning. However, the results may suggest that the strength of the impact gradually decreased with the shift from the individual level to project level and upward to the organizational level. Evidently, there are still opportunities to improve organizational learning practices in Aker BP.

9 Epilogue

9.1 Enabling learning in project-based organizations

This book combines a literature review and empirical findings from a longitudinal study of the Ivar Aasen project in order to identify and elaborate on the conditions that enable learning in project-based organizations. I have shown that learning takes place mainly through two interdependent processes:

- The process of learning within projects that is enabled by providing individuals and teams with possibilities in terms of time, suitable means and environments for experimentation, collective reflections, conceptualization, and exploration of the existing body of knowledge in the organization.
- The process of learning between projects that is enabled by providing individuals and teams with possibilities in terms of time and suitable means and environments for sharing and disseminating their own knowledge with other individuals and teams or with the wider organization.

The study findings suggested that several conditions had to be in place for the two interdependent processes of knowledge discovery, acquisition, sharing, dissemination, and reuse to take place:

- Individuals and teams should be provided with various types of meeting spaces, project review sessions or informal learning environments, such as communities of practices whereby members of the community interact with each other and share their experiences. These forums are critical for sharing tacit knowledge and procedural knowledge that are difficult to convert into explicit knowledge.

- The forums should provide opportunities for individuals to explain openly why sometimes things *have* gone wrong or right, not just what *can* go wrong or right.
- The meetings places should be arranged across projects on regular basis in order to encourage and emphasize the importance of sharing knowledge between individuals and teams. This should enable collective formulation of proven remedies, thus avoiding repetition of previous errors.
- Competence development programmes arranged by the organization should include sessions on lessons learned from previous projects, with the objective of presenting, discussing and comparing previously identified lessons with the experiences of the individuals attending the programmes.
- Physical space within projects should be planned to allow proximity between individuals and teams or to arrange for co-location of teams with mutual interdependency.
- Have a pool of experienced individuals in the organization who are willing and able to share their experiences with their colleagues through, for example, structured mentoring programmes, internal seminars or courses.
- Stronger emphasis should be placed on a more structured transfer of individuals between projects whenever possible.

All of the above conditions are examples of means that provides individuals with opportunities to express and share their opinions, ideas, lessons learned, engage in constructive confrontations, and challenge each other's viewpoints.

The study findings may suggest that learning and performance are not orthogonal dimensions that need to be balanced during project development, but are two mutually dependent parameters that have a circular relationship in such way that various activities related to learning contribute to improved performance. Improved performance contributes to greater appreciation of the role of learning in the project. The circular relationship between performance and learning could be supported by promoting and nurturing the following attitudes among individuals and teams:

- Encourage team members to recognize *interdependency between their tasks in projects and across projects*. This recognition is a precondition for expediting knowledge sharing in such a way that each team member will be able to perform their tasks in an optimum manner.

- Encourage team members to recognize their *own limitations and encourage individuals and teams to seek and ask for help* when needed, through direct contact, social network or other methods. According to many respondents in the study of the Ivar Aasen project, establishing *a culture that encourages knowledge seeking* is far more effective than introducing structured processes for capture and dissemination of knowledge.
- Encourage individuals and team members to not become *trapped with old habits* but rather to be open and receptive to new ideas and new concepts.
- Encourage individuals and team members to *challenge the established truths*, norms and the rules, and to seek to improve or change them.
- Create a work environment characterized by *psychological safety and tolerance for errors* in order to encourage experimentation, sharing and challenging the rules to find innovative solutions to complications or to challenges encountered during project development.
- Individuals regardless of their positions, seniority or organizational belonging should participate in various forms of project review sessions. Their participation is critical to understand the perspectives of the various parties involved in a project. Thus, facilitating the right balance between various opinions or views will lead to improved learning.

9.2 Improving systematic capture of lessons learned

In this subchapter I focus on discussing and elaborating on possible approaches to support knowledge capture from projects as an aid to support knowledge reuse between projects or to improve institutionalized level of learning. In this regard, I emphasize that knowledge capture through using, for example post-project reviews or other types of lessons-learned sessions, is not meant to be a substitute for the factors and enablers discussed in subchapter 9.1 but is meant to support the learning culture within the organization. There are three advantages of using systematic methods to capture lessons from projects.

First, according to Ellis and Davidi (2005), the application of formal lessons learned before after the action reviews sessions helps learners to switch their mode of information processing from automatic to conscious. In the automatic mode (e.g. casual discussions and conversations), people respond to external cues only in terms of their well-established, existing mental models. By contrast, in the conscious mode of information processing people's cognitive activity is characterized by greater awareness and more attention, information gathering and reflection.

Second, opportunities for social interaction across projects can be created between ongoing projects but are not applicable when there is a tangible time-lag between projects or when individuals leave their positions after completing the project. It should also be considered that moving individuals between projects to support social interaction is not always feasible, due to practical considerations and high turnover.

Third, from an organizational learning perspective, mindful articulation and the capture of lessons learned could provide hard evidence for questioning leadership styles, relations with suppliers, partners, and the customer base, as well as for questioning the existing project management processes in the organization.

9.3 Capturing reusable lessons learned

I have shown that lessons learned that have been captured from projects require revisions, screening and verification in order to facilitate their reuse in the future projects. However, my point of departure was that only individuals and teams working on future projects will be in a position to assess the applicability or usefulness of any lessons learned from previous projects. Hence, it is important that the lessons-learned process focuses on making it simpler for individuals working on future projects to make the assessment. The general approach adopted in this book has been to associate the lessons learned with the underlying characteristics of the project and its context. I have described the lessons-learned process in full, and have described the outcome of the process. In order to evaluate the lessons-learned process, I have drawn on the lessons learned from the Ivar Aasen project, and in Chapter 8 I have presented additional data from Aker BP to test the usefulness and applicability of the identified lessons learned.

9.4 Did we *really* learn?

The overall conclusions drawn from the analysis of the results obtained from the longitudinal study of the Ivar Aasen project suggest that the project not only manged to deliver its project objectives but also had a substantial impact on learning within the organization at both the individual level and the organizational level. In particular, the lessons learned from the Ivar Aasen project contributed to improvements in the following ways:

- Recognition of the advantages of collaboration and knowledge sharing
- Increased project competency at the individual level, team level and organizational level
- Provided valuable insights into the conditions of success in projects
- Provided confidence or strengthened the belief in success.

There is enough evidence to suggest that learning from Ivar Aasen is evident on the individual and group level. However, the study findings suggested that institutionalized level of learning still has some potential for improvement.

9.5 Suggestions for future research

More research is needed to investigate the circular relationship between performance and learning in projects. In this book, I have suggested a set of attitudes that could be used to establish and maintain the circular relationship between learning and performance. Further research is needed in order to identify additional attitudes or factors that influence this relationship.

In addition, performance is relatively easy to measure. There are well-known and established key performance indicators that could be monitored during the project in order to assess performance. However, during the project, it is difficult to answer the question *'Are we learning?'* or to evaluate the findings. Learning is a complex construct and is perceived differently by different people working on the same project. Hence, I believe that further understanding of how individuals and teams measure learning would improve our understanding of the circular relation between learning and performance.

In addition, the emergence of social media tools could provide wider and broader possibilities for sharing lessons learned in the organizations or across organizations. However, further studies are needed to assess the usefulness of such social media tools, both to improve inter-project learning and to improve intra-project learning.

Additionally, agile methods, due to their incremental nature, could provide better possibilities for improving project learning. Agile project methods have several increments with relatively short durations and are flexible in terms of scope development. Therefore, the methods focus more on knowledge sharing and collaboration by nature. Further studies are needed to assess the applicability of agile methods in large engineering projects, such as the Ivar Aasen project. We need to have a better understanding of the opportunities and limitations of the agile methods for improving learning in projects and across projects in large-scale engineering projects.

10 References

Aaltonen, K. and J. Kujala (2016). Towards an improved understanding of project stakeholder landscapes. *International Journal of Project Management, 34*(8): 1537–1552.

Aaltonen, K. and R. Sivonen (2009). Response strategies to stakeholder pressures in global projects. *International Journal of Project Management, 27*(2): 131–141.

Aerts, G., M. Dooms and E. Haezendonck (2017). Knowledge transfers and project-based learning in large scale infrastructure development projects: an exploratory and comparative ex-post analysis. *International Journal of Project Management, 35*(3): 224–240.

Ahmed, P.K., A.Y. Loh and M. Zairi (1999). Cultures for continuous improvement and learning. *Total Quality Management, 10*(4–5): 426–434.

Ajmal, M.M., T. Kekale and K.U. Koskinen (2009). Role of organisational culture for knowledge sharing in project environments. *International Journal of Project Organisation and Management, 1*(4): 358–374.

Al-Alawi, A.I., N.Y. Al-Marzooqi and Y.F. Mohammed (2007). Organizational culture and knowledge sharing: critical success factors. *Journal of Knowledge Management, 11*(2): 22–42.

Al-Hammad, A.-M. (2000). Common interface problems among various construction parties. *Journal of Performance of Constructed Facilities, 14*(2): 71–74.

Alveberg, L.-J. and E.V. Melberg (2013). Facts 2013: The Norwegian petroleum sector. *Ministry of Petroleum and Energy and Norwegian Petroleum Directorate.*

Alvesson, M. (2002). *Understanding Organizational Culture.* London, SAGE.

Anantatmula, V.S. (2010). Project manager leadership role in improving project performance. *Engineering Management Journal, 22*(1): 13–22.

Anbari, F.T., E.G. Carayannis and R.J. Voetsch (2008). Post-project reviews as a key project management competence. *Technovation, 28*(10): 633–643.

Antonacopoulou, E.P. (2006). The relationship between individual and organizational learning: new evidence from managerial learning practices. *Management Learning, 37*(4): 455–473.

Appelbaum, S. (2004). Organizational citizenship behavior: a case study of culture, leadership and trust. *Management Decision, 42*(1): 13–40.

Araujo, L. (1998). Knowing and learning as networking. *Management Learning, 29*(3): 317–336.

Argote, L., B. McEvily and R. Reagans (2003). Managing knowledge in organizations: an integrative framework and review of emerging themes. *Management Science, 49*(4): 571–582.

Argyris, C. (1977). Double loop learning in organizations. *Harvard Business Review, 55*(5): 115–125.

Argyris, C. and D. Schön (1997). Organizational learning: a theory of action perspective. *Reis*, (77/78), 345–348. DOI:10.2307/40183951

Armstrong, H. (2000). The learning organization: changed means to an unchanged end. *Organization, 7*(2): 355–361.

Arthur, M.B., R.J. DeFillippi and C. Jones (2001). Project-based learning as the interplay of career and company non-financial capital. *Management Learning, 32*(1): 99–117.

Artto, K.A., J.-M. Lehtonen and J. Saranen (2001). Managing projects front-end: incorporating a strategic early view to project management with simulation. *International Journal of Project Management, 19*(5): 255–264.

Atkinson, R. (1999). Project management: cost, time and quality, two best guesses and a phenomenon, its time to accept other success criteria. *International Journal of Project Management, 17*(6): 337–342.

Atkinson, R., L. Crawford and S. Ward (2006). Fundamental uncertainties in projects and the scope of project management. *International Journal of Project Management, 24*(8): 687–698.

Ayas, K. (1996). Professional project management: a shift towards learning and a knowledge creating structure. *International Journal of Project Management, 14*(3): 131–136.

Ayas, K. and N. Zeniuk (2001). Project-based learning: building communities of reflective practitioners. *Management Learning, 32*(1): 61–76.

Babb, J., R. Hoda and J. Nørbjerg (2014). Embedding reflection and learning into Agile software development. *IEEE Software, 31*(4): 51–57.

Bakker, R., J. Knoben, N. de Vries and L. Oerlemans (2011). The nature and prevalence of inter-organizational project ventures: evidence from a large scale field study in the Netherlands 2006–2009. *International Journal of Project Management, 29*(6): 781.

Balachandra, R. and J.H. Friar (1997). Factors for success in R&D projects and new product innovation: a contextual framework. *IEEE Transactions on Engineering Management, 44*(3): 276–287.

Bartsch, V., M. Ebers and I. Maurer (2013). Learning in project-based organizations: the role of project teams' social capital for overcoming barriers to learning. *International Journal of Project Management, 31*(2): 239–251.

Bass, B.M. and R.E. Riggio (2006). *Transformational Leadership.* Mahwah, NJ, L. Erlbaum Associates.

Basten, D. and T. Haamann (2018). Approaches for organizational learning: a literature review. *SAGE Open, 8*(3). DOI:10/1177/2158244018794224

Behringer, N. and K. Sassenberg (2015). Introducing social media for knowledge management: determinants of employees' intentions to adopt new tools. *Computers in Human Behavior, 48*: 290–296.

Belassi, W., A.Z. Kondra and O.I. Tukel (2007). New product development projects: the effects of organizational culture. *Project Management Journal, 38*(4): 12–24.

Benner, M.J. and M.L. Tushman (2003). Exploitation, exploration, and process management: the productivity dilemma revisited. *Academy of Management Review, 28*(2): 238–256.

Bennett, B. (2003). Job rotation: its role in promoting learning in organizations. *Development and Learning in Organizations, 17*(4): 7–9.

Berwick, D. M. (1996). A primer on leading the improvement of systems. *BMJ, 312*(7031): 619–622.

Blake, R.R. (1969). *Building a Dynamic Corporation Through Grid Organization Development.* Reading, MA: Addison-Wesley.

Blindenbach-Driessen, F. and J. van den Ende (2006). Innovation in project-based firms: the context dependency of success factors. *Research Policy, 35*(4): 545–561.

Børve, S., T. Ahola, B. Andersen and W. Aarseth (2017). Partnering in offshore drilling projects. *International Journal of Managing Projects in Business, 10*(1): 84–108.

Boud, D. and D. Walker (1998). Promoting reflection in professional courses: the challenge of context. *Studies in Higher Education, 23*(2): 191–206.

Brady, T. and A. Davies (2004). Building project capabilities: from exploratory to exploitative learning. *Organization Studies, 25*(9): 1601–1621.

Brady, T., N. Marshall, A. Prencipe and F. Tell (2002). *Making sense of learning landscapes in project-based organizations.* Third European Conference on Organizational Knowledge, Learning and Capabilities, 5–6 April 2002, Athens, Greece.

Bresnen, M. (2006). Conflicting and conflated discourses? Project management, organisational change and learning. In D. Hodgson and S. Cicmil (eds.), *Making Projects Critical* (pp. 68–89). Basingstoke: Palgrave Macmillan.

Busby, J.S. (1999a). An assessment of post-project reviews. *Project Management Journal, 30*(3): 23–29.

Busby, J.S. (1999b). The effectiveness of collective retrospection as a mechanism of organizational learning. *The Journal of Applied Behavioral Science, 35*(1): 109–129.

Caldwell, R. (2012). Leadership and learning: a critical reexamination of Senge's learning organization. *Systemic Practice and Action Research, 25*(1): 39–55.

Carrillo, P., K. Ruikar and P. Fuller (2013). When will we learn? Improving lessons learned practice in construction. *International Journal of Project Management, 31*(4): 567–578.

Cavaleri, S.A. and D.S. Fearon (2000). Integrating organizational learning and business praxis: a case for intelligent project management. *The Learning Organization, 7*(5): 251–258.

Chan, A.P.C., D. Scott and A.P.L. Chan (2004). Factors affecting the success of a construction project. *Journal of Construction Engineering and Management, 130*(1): 153–155.

Chang, A.S.-T. (2002). Reasons for cost and schedule increase for engineering design projects. *Journal of Management in Engineering, 18*(1): 29–36.

Chen, G., G. Zhang, Y.-M. Xie and X.-H. Jin (2012). Overview of alliancing research and practice in the construction industry. *Architectural Engineering and Design Management, 8*(2): 103–119.

Chiva, R. and J. Alegre (2005). Organizational learning and organizational knowledge: towards the integration of two approaches. *Management Learning, 36*(1): 49–68.

Chua, D.K. and M. Godinot (2006). Use of a WBS matrix to improve interface management in projects. *Journal of Construction Engineering and Management, 132*(1): 67–79.

Cohen, W.M. and D.A. Levinthal (1990). Absorptive capacity: a new perspective on learning and innovation. *Administrative Science Quarterly, 35*(1): 128–152.

Collier, B., T. DeMarco and P. Fearey (1996). A defined process for project post mortem review. *IEEE Software, 13*(4): 65–72.

Collins, A. and D. Baccarini (2004). Project success – A survey. *Journal of Construction Research, 5*(2): 211–231.

Cooke, R.A. and J.L. Szumal (1993). Measuring normative beliefs and shared behavioral expectations in organizations: the reliability and validity of the Organizational Culture Inventory. *Psychological Reports, 72*(3): 1299–1330.

Cooke-Davies, T. (2002). The 'real' success factors on projects. *International Journal of Project Management, 20*(3): 185–190.

Crossan, M.M., H.W. Lane and R.E. White (1999). An organizational learning framework: from intuition to institution. *Academy of Management Review, 24*(3): 522–537.

Damm, D. and M. Schindler (2002). Security issues of a knowledge medium for distributed project work. *International Journal of Project Management, 20*(1): 37–47.

Das, T.K. and T. Bing-Sheng (1998). Between trust and control: developing confidence in partner cooperation in alliances. *The Academy of Management Review, 23*(3): 491–512.

Davenport, T.H. and L. Prusak (1998). *Working Knowledge: How Organizations Manage What They Know.* Boston, MA: Harvard Business Press.

Davidson, J. (2006). Finding the value in lessons learned databases. *Knowledge Management Review, 9*(3): 6–7.

DeFillippi, R.J. (2001). Introduction: project-based learning, reflective practices and learning. *Management Learning, 32*(1): 5–10.

de Vries, M.F.R.K. and D. Miller (1984). *The Neurotic Organization: Diagnosing and Changing Counterproductive Styles of Management.* Hoboken, NJ: Jossey-Bass.

de Wit, A. (1988). Measurement of project success. *International Journal of Project Management, 6*(3): 164–170.

Disterer, G. (2002). Management of project knowledge and experiences. *Journal of Knowledge Management, 6*(5): 512–520.

Dixon, N.M. (2017). *The Organizational Learning Cycle: How We Can Learn Collectively.* London: Routledge.

Duffield, S. and S.J. Whitty (2015). Developing a systemic lessons learned knowledge model for organisational learning through projects. *International Journal of Project Management, 33*(2): 311–324.

Duhon, H.J. and J.S. Elias (2008). Why it is difficult to learn lessons: insights from decision theory and cognitive science. *SPE Projects, Facilities & Construction, 3*(03): 1–7.

Dybå, T., T. Dingsøyr and N.B. Moe (2014). Agile project management. In G. Ruhe and C. Wohlin (eds.), *Software Project Management in a Changing World* (pp. 277–300). Berlin, Heidelberg: Springer.

Easterby-Smith, M., M. Crossan and D. Nicolini (2000). Organizational learning: debates past, present and future. *Journal of Management Studies, 37*(6): 783–796.

Easterby-Smith, M. and M.A. Lyles (2011). *Handbook of Organizational Learning and Knowledge Management.* Wiley Online Library. DOI:10.1002/9781119207245

Edmondson, A.C. (2003). Managing the risk of learning: psychological safety in work teams. In M. West, D. Tjosvold and K.G. Smith (eds.), *International Handbook of Organizational Teamwork and Cooperative Working* (pp. 255–276). London: John Wiley & Sons.

Edmondson, A. (2004). Psychological safety, trust, and learning in organizations: a group-level lens. In M. Kramer and K.S. Cook (eds.), *Trust and Distrust in*

Organizations: Dilemmas and Approaches (pp. 239–272). New York: Russel Sage Foundation.

Edmondson, A. and B. Moingeon (1999). Learning, trust and organizational change. In M. Easterby-Smith, J. Burgoyne and L. Araujo (eds.), *Organizational Learning and the Learning Organization* (pp. 157–175). London: SAGE.

Edmondson, A.C. (2011). Strategies for learning from failure. *Harvard Business Review, 89*(4): 48–55.

Ekrot, B., A. Kock and H.G. Gemünden (2016). Retaining project management competence – antecedents and consequences. *International Journal of Project Management, 34*(2): 145–157.

Elkjaer, B. (2003). Social learning theory: learning as participation in social processes. In M. Easterby-Smith and M.A. Lyles (eds.), *Blackwell Handbook of Organizational Learning and Knowledge Management* (pp. 38–53). Malden, MA: Blackwell.

Ellis, S. (2012). Learning from errors: the role of after-event reviews. In J. Bauer and C. Harteis (eds.), *Human Fallibility: The Ambiguity of Errors for Work and Learning* (vol. 6, pp. 215–232). Dordrecht: Springer Netherlands.

Ellis, S. and I. Davidi (2005). After-event reviews: drawing lessons from successful and failed experience. *Journal of Applied Psychology, 90*(5): 857–871.

Ellison, N.B., J.L. Gibbs and M.S. Weber (2015). The use of enterprise social network sites for knowledge sharing in distributed organizations: the role of organizational affordances. *American Behavioral Scientist, 59*(1): 103–123.

Errasti, A., R. Beach, A. Oyarbide and J. Santos (2007). A process for developing partnerships with subcontractors in the construction industry: an empirical study. *International Journal of Project Management, 25*(3): 250–256.

Fillion, G., V. Koffi and J.P.B. Ekionea (2015). Peter Senge's learning organization: a critical view and the addition of some new concepts to actualize theory and practice. *Journal of Organizational Culture, Communications and Conflict, 19*(3): 73–102.

Fiol, C.M. and M.A. Lyles (1985). Organizational learning. *The Academy of Management Review, 10*(4): 803–813.

Foss, N.J. and P.H. Christensen (2011). Utfordringer ved motivasjon og ledelse av kunnskaparbeidere. *Magma* (3): 41–48.

Fuller, P. (2011). *Improving Lessons in Multi-phase Project Environments*. PhD thesis. Loughborough University.

Gaál, Z., L. Szabó, N. Obermayer-Kovács and A. Csepregi (2015). Exploring the role of social media in knowledge sharing. *Electronic Journal of Knowledge Management, 13*(3): 185–197.

GAO. (2002). *NASA: Better Mechanisms Needed for Sharing Lessons Learned.* GAO-02-195. Washington DC: United States General Accounting Office.

Garvin, D.A. (1993) Building a learning organization. *Harvard Business Review, 71*(4): 78–91.

Gersick, C.J. (1988). Time and transition in work teams: toward a new model of group development. *Academy of Management Journal, 31*(1): 9–41.

Gherardi, S. and D. Nicolini (2000). To transfer is to transform: the circulation of safety knowledge. *Organization, 7*(2): 329–348.

Goffee, R. and G. Jones (1998). *The Character of a Corporation: How Your Company's Culture Can Make or Break Your Business.* New York: Harper Business.

Grabher, G. (2002). The project ecology of advertising: tasks, talents and teams. *Regional Studies, 36*(3): 245–262.

Grace, T.P.L. (2009). Wikis as a knowledge management tool. *Journal of Knowledge Management, 10*(4): 64–74.

Hannah, S.T. and P.B. Lester (2009). A multilevel approach to building and leading learning organizations. *The Leadership Quarterly, 20*(1): 34–48.

Hara, N. and T.M. Schwen (2006). Communities of practice in workplaces. *Performance Improvement Quarterly, 19*(2): 93–114.

Hartmann, A. and A. Dorée (2015). Learning between projects: more than sending messages in bottles. *International Journal of Project Management, 33*(2): 341–351.

Hietajärvi, A.-M., K. Aaltonen and H. Haapasalo (2017). Managing integration in infrastructure alliance projects: dynamics of integration mechanisms. *International Journal of Managing Projects in Business, 10*(1): 5–31.

Hobday, M. (2000). The project-based organisation: an ideal form for managing complex products and systems? *Research Policy, 29*(7–8): 871–893.

Hoffmann, W.H. and R. Schlosser (2001). Success factors of strategic alliances in small and medium-sized enterprises—an empirical survey. *Long Range Planning, 34*(3): 357–381.

Hofstede, G. (1991). *Cultures and Organizations: Software of the Mind.* London: McGraw-Hill.

Huber, G.P. (1991). Organizational learning: the contributing processes and the literatures. *Organization Science, 2*(1): 88–115.

Hussein, B. (2018). *The Road to Success: Narratives and Insights from Real-life Projects.* Bergen: Fagbokforlaget.

Hussein, B., A. Mallcott and N. Mikhridinova (2019). Lessons learned from developing and applying self-assessment instruments for evaluating project management competences in two large organizations. *Procedia Computer Science, 164*: 358–365.

Hutchinson, A. and J. Gallagher (2003). *Project Alliances: An Overview*. Melbourne: Aichimie Pty and Phillips Fox Lawyers.

Inkpen, A.C. and S.C. Currall (2004). The coevolution of trust, control, and learning in joint ventures. *Organization Science, 15*(5): 586–599.

Jarrahi, M.H. and S. Sawyer (2013). Social technologies, informal knowledge practices, and the enterprise. *Journal of Organizational Computing and Electronic Commerce, 23*(1–2): 110–137.

Jasimuddin, S.M. and Z.P. Zhang (2014). Knowledge management strategy and organizational culture. *Journal of the Operational Research Society, 65*(10): 1490–1500.

Jergeas, G.F. (2008). Analysis of the front-end loading of Alberta mega oil sands projects. *Project Management Journal, 39*(4): 95–104.

Jugdev, K. and R. Müller (2005). A retrospective look at our evolving understanding of project success. *Project Management Journal, 36*(4): 19–31.

Jønsson, T. and H.J. Jeppesen (2013). Under the influence of the team? An investigation of the relationships between team autonomy, individual autonomy and social influence within teams. *International Journal of Human Resource Management, 24*(1): 78–93.

Kadefors, A. (2004). Trust in project relationships—inside the black box. *International Journal of Project Management, 22*(3): 175–182.

Keegan, A. and J.R. Turner (2001). Quantity versus quality in project-based learning practices. *Management Learning, 32*(1): 77–98.

Kerzner, H. (2013). *Project Management: A Systems Approach to Planning, Scheduling, and Controlling*. Hoboken, NJ: Wiley.

Kim, D.H. (1993). The link between individual and organizational learning. *Sloan Management Review, 35*: 37–50.

Kogut, B. (1988). Joint ventures: theoretical and empirical perspectives. *Strategic Management Journal, 9*(4): 319–332.

Kolb, D.A. (1984). *Experiential Learning: Experience as the Source of Learning and Development*. Englewood Cliffs, NJ: Prentice-Hall.

Koners, U. and K. Goffin (2007). Learning from postproject reviews: a cross-case analysis. *Journal of Product Innovation Management, 24*(3): 242–258.

Koskinen, K.U., P. Pihlanto and H. Vanharanta (2003). Tacit knowledge acquisition and sharing in a project work context. *International Journal of Project Management, 21*(4): 281–290.

Kotnour, T. (2000). Organizational learning practices in the project management environment. *International Journal of Quality & Reliability Management, 17*(4/5): 393–406.

Kotnour, T. and C. Vergopia (2005). Learning-based project reviews: observations and lessons learned from the Kennedy Space Center. *Engineering Management Journal, 17*(4): 30–38.

Kransdorff, A. (1996). Viewpoint: using the benefits of hindsight – the role of post-project analysis. *Managerial Auditing Journal, 11*(4): 42–46.

Kvale, S. and Brinkmann, S. (2009). *Interviews: learning the craft of qualitative research interviewing* (2nd ed.). Los Angeles, CA: Sage.

Langfred, C.W. (2004). Too much of a good thing? Negative effects of high trust and individual autonomy in self-managing teams. *Academy of Management Journal, 47*(3): 385–399.

Lau, E. and S. Rowlinson (2011). The implications of trust in relationships in managing construction projects. *International Journal of Managing Projects in Business, 4*(4): 633–659.

Leonard, D. and W. Swap (2005). *Deep Smarts: How to Cultivate and Transfer Enduring Business Wisdom.* Boston, MA: Harvard Business Review Press.

Leonardi, P.M. (2017). The social media revolution: Sharing and learning in the age of leaky knowledge. *Information and Organization, 27*(1): 47–59.

Leung, M.-Y., A. Chong, S.T. Ng and M.C.K. Cheung (2004). Demystifying stakeholders' commitment and its impacts on construction projects. *Construction Management and Economics, 22*(7): 701–715.

Lieberman, D.A. (2012). *Human Learning and Memory.* New York: Cambridge University Press.

Liebowitz, J. (2005). Conceptualizing and implementing knowledge management. In P.E.D. Love, P.S.W. Fong and Z. Irani (eds.), *Management of Knowledge in Project Environments* (pp. 1–18). Oxford: Butterworth-Heinemann.

Lindner, F. and A. Wald (2011). Success factors of knowledge management in temporary organizations. *International Journal of Project Management, 29*(7): 877–888.

Loosemore, M. (2006). *Risk Management in Projects.* London and New York: Tayor & Francis.

Love, P.E.D. and A. Gunasekaran (1999). Learning alliances: a customer-supplier focus for continuous improvement in manufacturing. *Industrial and Commercial Training, 31*(3): 88–96.

Love, P.E.D., P.S.W. Fong and Z. Irani (2005). *Management of Knowledge in Project Environments.* Amsterdam: Butterworth Heinemann.

Love, P.E.D., Z. Irani and D.J. Edwards (2003). learning to reduce rework in projects: analysis of firm's organizational learning and quality practices. *Project Management Journal, 34*(3): 13–25.

Lucas, C. and T. Kline (2008). Understanding the influence of organizational culture and group dynamics on organizational change and learning. *The Learning Organization, 15*(3): 277–287.

March, J.G. (1991). Exploration and exploitation in organizational learning. *Organization Science, 2*(1): 71–87.

March, J.G., L.S. Sproull and M. Tamuz (1991). Learning from samples of one or fewer. *Organization Science, 2*(1): 1–13.

Marsick, V.J. and K.E. Watkins (2003). Demonstrating the value of an organization's learning culture: the dimensions of the learning organization questionnaire. *Advances in Developing Human Resources, 5*(2): 132–151.

Matschke, C., J. Moskaliuk, F. Bokhorst, T. Schümmer and U. Cress (2014). Motivational factors of information exchange in social information spaces. *Computers in Human Behavior, 36*: 549–558.

Mayo, A. and E. Lank (1994). *The Power of Learning: A Guide to Gaining Competitive Advantage.* London: Chartered Institute of Personnel & Development.

McClory, S., M. Read and A. Labib (2017). Conceptualising the lessons-learned process in project management: towards a triple-loop learning framework. *International Journal of Project Management, 35*(7): 1322–1335.

McGill, M.E. and J.W. Slocum (1993). Unlearning the organization. *Organizational Dynamics, 22*(2): 67–79.

McLeod, L. and S.G. MacDonell (2011). Factors that affect software systems development project outcomes. *ACM Computing Surveys, 43*(4): 1–56.

Michell, V. and J. McKenzie (2017). Lessons learned. *VINE Journal of Information and Knowledge Management Systems, 47*(3): 411–428.

Milosevic, D.Z. (1990). Case study: integrating the owner's and the contractor's project organization. *Project Management Journal, 21*(4): 23.

Milton, N. (2010). *The Lessons Learned Handbook: Practical Approaches to Learning from Experience.* Oxford: Chandos Publishing.

Moingeon, B. and A. Edmondson (1998). Trust and organizational learning. In N. Lazaric and E. Lorenz (eds.), *Trust and Economic Learning* (pp. 228–247). Cheltenham: Edward Elgar.

Moskaliuk, J. and J. Kimmerle (2009). Using wikis for organizational learning: functional and psycho-social principles. *Development and Learning in Organizations, 23*(4): 21–24.

Mueller, J. (2014). A specific knowledge culture: cultural antecedents for knowledge sharing between project teams. *European Management Journal, 32*(2): 190–202.

Müller, R. and R. Turner (2010). Leadership competency profiles of successful project managers. *International Journal of Project Management, 28*(5): 437.

NATO. (2011). *The NATO Lessons Learned Handbook.* Norfolk, VA: NATO, Joint Analysis and Lessons Learned Centre.

Newell, S. and L.F. Edelman (2008). Developing a dynamic project learning and cross-project learning capability: synthesizing two perspectives. *Information Systems Journal,* 18(6): 567–591.

Newell, S., M. Bresnen, L. Edelman, H. Scarbrough and J. Swan (2006). Sharing knowledge across projects: limits to ICT-led project review practices. *Management Learning,* 37(2): 167–185.

Nijhof, W.J., M.J. de Jong and G. Beukhof (1998). Employee commitment in changing organizations: an exploration. *Journal of European Industrial Training,* 22(6): 243–248.

Nonaka, I. (1991). The knowledge creating company. *Harvard Business Review,* 69: 96–104.

Nonaka, I. and H. Takeuchi. (1995). *The Knowledge-Creating Company: How Japanese Companies Create the Dynamics of Innovation.* New York: Oxford University Press.

Nooteboom, U. (2004). Interface management improves on-time, on-budget delivery of megaprojects. *Journal of Petroleum Technology,* 56(08): 32–34.

Norwegianpetroleum. (2020). Goverenment's revenues. Retrieved from https://www.norskpetroleum.no/en/economy/governments-revenues/

Oldham, G. R. and J.R. Hackman (2010). Not what it was and not what it will be: the future of job design research. *Journal of Organizational Behavior,* 31: 463–479.

Oliver, S. and K. Kondal Reddy (2006). How to develop knowledge culture in organizations? A multiple case study of large distributed organizations. *Journal of Knowledge Management,* 10(4): 6–24.

Orlikowski, W.J. (2006). Material knowing: the scaffolding of human knowledgeability. *European Journal of Information Systems,* 15(5): 460–466.

Örtenblad, A. (2001). On differences between organizational learning and learning organization. *The Learning Organization,* 8(3): 125–133.

Palanski, M.E., S.S. Kahai and F.J. Yammarino (2011). Team virtues and performance: an examination of transparency, behavioral integrity, and trust. *Journal of Business Ethics,* 99(2): 201–216.

Park, H., V. Ribière and W.D. Schulte (2004). Critical attributes of organizational culture that promote knowledge management technology implementation success. *Journal of Knowledge Management,* 8(3): 106–117.

Paroutis, S. and A. Al Saleh (2009). Determinants of knowledge sharing using Web 2.0 technologies. *Journal of Knowledge Management,* 13(4): 52–63.

Pavitt, T. and A. Gibb (2003). Interface management within construction: in particular, building façade. *Journal of Construction Engineering and Management, 129*(1): 8–15.

Perminova, O., M. Gustafsson and K. Wikstrom (2008). Defining uncertainty in projects – a new perspective. *International Journal of Project Management, 26*(1): 73–79.

Phillips, B.T. (2003). A four-level learning organisation benchmark implementation model. *The Learning Organization, 10*(2): 98–105.

Pinto, J.K. (2012). *Project Management: Achieving Competitive Advantage.* Boston, MA: Prentice Hall.

Pinto, J., D. Slevin and B. English (2009). Trust in projects: an empirical assessment of owner/contractor relationships. *International Journal of Project Management, 27*(6): 638–648.

Pirkkalainen, H. and J.M. Pawlowski (2014). Global social knowledge management–understanding barriers for global workers utilizing social software. *Computers in Human Behavior, 30*: 637–647.

Polanyi, M. (1966). The logic of tacit inference. *Philosophy, 41*(155): 1–18.

Prencipe, A. and F. Tell (2001). Inter-project learning: processes and outcomes of knowledge codification in project-based firms. *Research Policy, 30*(9): 1373–1394.

Prince, M.J. and R.M. Felder (2006). Inductive teaching and learning methods: definitions, comparisons, and research bases. *Journal of Engineering Education, 95*(2): 123–138.

Project Management Institute. (2013). *A Guide to the Project Management Body of Knowledge (PMBOK® Guide).* 5th ed. Newton Square, PA: Project Management Institute.

Rabkin, D.G. (1995). *The role of explication in noticing: the discovery and use of new variables in decision making* (unpublished doctoral dissertation). Massachusetts Institute of Technology, Sloan School of Management.

Rai, R.K. (2011). Knowledge management and organizational culture: a theoretical integrative framework. *Journal of Knowledge Management, 15*(5): 779–801.

Rebelo, T.M. and A.D. Gomes (2011). Conditioning factors of an organizational learning culture. *Journal of Workplace Learning, 23*(3): 173–194.

Revans, R. (2017). *ABC of Action Learning.* Taylor and Francis. DOI: 10.4324/9781315263533.

Ringdal, K. (2007). *Enhet og mangfold: Samfunnsvitenskapelig forskning og kvantitativ metode.* Bergen: Fagbokforlaget.

Robson, C. (2011). *Real World Research: A Resource for Users of Social Research Methods in Applied Settings.* Chichester: Wiley.

Rolstadås, A., J. Pinto, P. Falster and R. Venkataraman (2014). *Decision Making in Project Management*. Bergen: Fagbokforlaget.

Rose, A.-L., J. Dee and L. Leisyte (2020). Organizational learning through projects: a case of a German university. *The Learning Organization, 27*(2): 85–99.

Rowlinson, S., F.Y. Cheung, R. Simons and A. Rafferty (2006). Alliancing in Australia—no-litigation contracts: a tautology? *Journal of Professional Issues in Engineering Education and Practice, 132*(1): 77–81.

Santos, R.E.S., F.Q.B. da Silva and C.V.C. da Magalhães (2016). *Benefits and Limitations of Job Rotation in Software Organizations: A Systematic Literature Review*. Limerick: Association for Computing Machinery.

Scarbrough, H., J. Swan, S. Laurent, M. Bresnen, L. Edelman and S. Newell (2004). Project-based learning and the role of learning boundaries. *Organization Studies, 25*(9): 1579–1600.

Schein, E.H. (1990). *Organizational Culture and Leadership*. San Francisco, CA: Jossey-Bass.

Schein, E.H. (2010). *Organizational Culture and Leadership*. Hoboken, NJ: John Wiley.

Schindler, M. and M.J. Eppler (2003). Harvesting project knowledge: a review of project learning methods and success factors. *International Journal of Project Management, 21*(3): 219–228.

Schön, D. and C. Argyris (1996). *Organizational Learning II: Theory, Method and Practice*. Reading, MA: Addison-Wesley.

Schwab, A. (2007). Incremental organizational learning from multilevel information sources: evidence for cross-level interactions. *Organization Science, 18*(2): 233–251.

Secchi, P., R. Ciaschi and D. Spence (1999). A concept for an ESA lessons learned system. In P. Secchi (ed.), *Alerts and Lessons Learned: An Effective Way to Prevent Failures and Problems* (pp. 57–61). Noordwijk: ESTEC.

Senge, P.M. (1990). *The Fifth Discipline: The Art and Practice of The Learning Organization*. New York: Doubleday.

Sense, A.J. (2007). Structuring the project environment for learning. *International Journal of Project Management, 25*(4): 405–412.

Sense, A.J. (2011). The project workplace for organizational learning development. *International Journal of Project Management, 29*(8): 986–993.

Sense, A.J. and M. Antoni (2003). Exploring the politics of project learning. *International Journal of Project Management, 21*(7): 487–494.

Shaw, D. (2017). Managing people and learning in organisational change projects. *Journal of Organizational Change Management, 30*(6): 923–935.

Shenhar, A.J., D. Milosevic, D. Dvir and H. Thamhain (2007). *Linking Project Management to Business Strategy.* Newtown Square, PA: Project Management Institute.

Shokri, S., M. Safa, C.T. Haas, R.C.G. Haas, K. Maloney and S. MacGillivray (2012). *Interface Management Model for Mega Capital Projects.* Construction Research Congress 2012. West Lafayette, IN: American Society of Civil Engineers.

Shokri-Ghasabeh, M. and N. Chileshe (2014). Knowledge management: barriers to capturing lessons learned from Australian construction contractors perspective. *Construction Innovation, 14*(1): 108–134.

Siddique, L. and B.A. Hussein (2016). A qualitative study of success criteria in Norwegian agile software projects from suppliers' perspective. *International Journal of Information Systems and Project Management, 4*(2): 65–79.

Siddique, L. and B.A. Hussein (2019). Enablers and barriers to customer involvement in agile software projects in Norwegian software industry: the supplier's perspective. *The Journal of Modern Project Management, 7*(2). DOI:10.19255/jmpm395

Simon, H.A. (1969). *The Sciences of the Artificial.* Cambridge, MA: MIT.

Smyth, H. and A. Edkins (2007). Relationship management in the management of PFI/PPP projects in the UK. *International Journal of Project Management, 25*(3): 232–240.

Smyth, H., M. Gustafsson and E. Ganskau (2010). The value of trust in project business. *International Journal of Project Management, 28*(2): 117–129.

Song, X.M. and M.E. Parry (1997). Teamwork barriers in Japanese high-technology firms: the sociocultural differences between R&D and marketing managers. *Journal of Product Innovation Management, 14*(5): 356–367.

Stata, R. (1989). Organizational Learning: The Key to Management Innovation. *Sloan Management Review, 30*(3): 63.

Swan, J., H. Scarbrough and S. Newell (2010). Why don't (or do) organizations learn from projects? *Management Learning, 41*(3): 325–344.

Swan, J., H. Scarbrough and M. Robertson (2002). The construction of 'communities of practice' in the management of innovation. *Management Learning, 33*(4): 477–496.

Sydow, J., L. Lindkvist and R. DeFillippi (2004). Project-based organizations, embeddedness and repositories of knowledge. [Editorial] *Organization Studies, 25*(9): 1475–1489.

Thagaard, T. (2008). *Systematikk og innlevelse.* Bergen: Fagbokforlaget.

Tishler, A., D. Dvir, A. Shenhar and S. Lipovetsky (1996). Identifying critical success factors in defense development projects: a multivariate analysis. *Technological Forecasting and Social Change, 51*(2): 151–171.

Tsang, E.W.K. (1997). Organizational learning and the learning organization: a dichotomy between descriptive and prescriptive research. *Human Relations, 50*(1): 73–89.

Turner, J.R., A.E. Keegan and L. Crawford (2000). *Learning by experience in the project-based organization*. Paper presented at PMI® Research Conference 2000: Project Management Research at the Turn of the Millennium, Paris, France. Newtown Square, PA: Project Management Institute.

Turner, R.J. (2009). *The Handbook of Project-based Management: Leading Strategic Change in Organizations.* New York: McGraw-Hill.

van Donk, D.P. and J. Riezebos (2005). Exploring the knowledge inventory in project-based organisations: a case study. *International Journal of Project Management, 23*(1): 75–83.

van Wyk, R., P. Bowen and A. Akintoye (2008). Project risk management practice: the case of a South African utility company. *International Journal of Project Management, 26*(2): 149–163.

Vera, D. and M. Crossan (2004). Strategic leadership and organizational learning. *Academy of Management Review, 29*(2): 222–240.

Vergopia, C. (2008). *Project Review Maturity and Project Performance: An Empirical Case Study.* Orlando, Florida: University of Central Florida.

Von Zedtwitz, M. (2002). Organizational learning through post–project reviews in R&D. *R&D Management, 32*(3): 255–268.

Weber, R., D.W. Aha and I. Becerra-Fernandez (2001). Intelligent lessons learned systems. *Expert Systems with Applications, 20*(1): 17–34.

Wenger, E. (1998). *Communities of Practice: Learning, Meaning, and Identity.* Cambridge UK: Cambridge University Press.

Wiewiora, A., G. Murphy, B. Trigunarsyah and K. Brown (2014). Interactions between organizational culture, trustworthiness, and mechanisms for inter-project knowledge sharing. *Project Management Journal, 45*(2): 48–65.

Wiewiora, A., M. Smidt and A. Chang (2019). The 'how' of multilevel learning dynamics: a systematic literature review exploring how mechanisms bridge learning between individuals, teams/projects and the organization. *European Management Review, 16*(1): 93–115.

Williams, T. (2007). *Post Project Reviews to Gain Effective Lessons Learned.* Newtown Square, PA: Project Management Institute.

Williams, T. (2008). How do organizations learn lessons from projects—and do they? *IEEE Transactions on Engineering Management, 55*(2): 248–266.

Williams, T. and K. Samset (2010). Issues in front-end decision making on projects. *Project Management Journal, 41*(2): 38–49.

Yazici, H.J. (2009). The role of project management maturity and organizational culture in perceived performance. *Project Management Journal, 40*(3): 14–33.

Yeung, J.F.Y., A.P.C. Chan and D.W.M. Chan (2007). The definition of alliancing in construction as a Wittgenstein family-resemblance concept. *International Journal of Project Management, 25*(3): 219–231.

Zaghloul, R. and F. Hartman (2003). Construction contracts: the cost of mistrust. *International Journal of Project Management, 21*(6): 419–424.

Zheng, W., B. Yang and G.N. McLean (2010). Linking organizational culture, structure, strategy, and organizational effectiveness: mediating role of knowledge management. *Journal of Business Research, 63*(7): 763–771.

Zollo, M. and S.G. Winter (2002). Deliberate learning and the evolution of dynamic capabilities. *Organization Science, 13*(3): 339–351.

Zwikael, O. and M. Ahn (2011). The effectiveness of risk management: an analysis of project risk planning across industries and countries. *Risk Analysis, 31*(1): 25–37.

11 Appendixes

11.1 Appendix 1: Questionnaire – Subprojects

Question 1. Work tasks
The scope of the work
The technological challenges in the subproject
Organizational challenges (contributors/suppliers/subcontractors) and the need for interface/communication between contributors

Question 2. Success factors
From a holistic perspective and from your own experience, what were the most important challenges in your subproject?
What factors do you think have contributed to success in your subproject? What could have been handled in a better way?
Highlight only one condition that you think has been crucial to success in your subproject. What is it, and why has it been crucial?
What is the most important thing you have learned as a project manager in your subproject?

Question 3. Implementation frameworks
Describe the most important guidelines and priorities that you were asked to adhere to in your subproject.
Were these guidelines and limitations understandable to you right from the start?
How important to you as a project manager was it to have a good understanding of these guidelines and limitations right from the start?

Describe a situation or event when these limitations or guidelines have been very demanding, but when you were able to respond with a solution. What have you learned from this story?
What can we learn?

Question 4. Complexity
How would you rate the complexity of your subproject (technological, organizational cultural)?
Can you describe any situations (problems and challenges) that have arisen because of this complexity? What did you need as a project manager?
How can we prevent problems caused by complexity? What actions can we take to prevent these problems?

Question 5. People and relationships
People play a very central role in projects. The project director expects efforts and dedication from all to achieve the project goals.
What have you done to make people do their best? What was your approach?
How did you work to maintain motivation, trust, and dedication among your team members?
How did the project team respond to your actions/approach?
What is your advice for new project managers with regard to collaborating with the people in the project? What works best? What does not work?
Can you, based on your experience of your project, describe what kind of project manager is required?

Question 6. Uncertainty
Uncertainty (lack of adequate information/knowledge or confusion about expectations, scope of work, roles, and responsibilities).
Have you been unsure as to how your task in the project should be solved? If so, what have you been unsure about?
How has this uncertainty affected you as a project manager? What have you done to deal with this uncertainty?
If you were to advise forthcoming project managers on how to relate to the uncertainty, what would you say? What personal attributes are required to cope with the uncertainty?

Question 7. Relations with senior management and/or project management

How did you experience follow-up and support from top management in the project?

What advice would you like to provide to management with regard to improvements?

What norms and values governed the implementation of this project?

11.2 Appendix 2. Questionnaire – Supporting functions

Question 1. Success factors
From a holistic perspective and from your own experience, identify the most important challenges with regard to your tasks and your relationship with different project managers/managers.
What factors do you think have contributed to the success of your work? What conditions could have been taken into account in a better way?
List only one factor that you believe has been crucial to success in your work. Why?
What is the most important lesson you have learned from your work in the project?

Question 2. Relations with senior management and/or subproject managers
What was most demanding with regard to interacting with other project managers/subproject managers?
Have you been unsure about your tasks in the project, or about relationships with other project participants? If so, what have you been unsure of? How has this uncertainty affected you? What have you done to deal with this uncertainty?
Can you describe a situation or event when this uncertainty was very demanding? How did you manage to cope with this situation? What have you learned from this experience?
Based on your experience of your role in the project, can you describe the type of person required for the job? What skills and personal qualities are required?
How did you experience follow-up and support from top management in the project?
What advice would you give top management?
Is there anything else you would like to add?

11.3   Appendix 3. Questionnaire – Project management

Question 1. Challenges
From a holistic perspective and from your own experience, identify the most important challenges regarding your relationship with:
Subproject managers
The management of Det norske/Aker BP
Suppliers
Subcontractors
Partnership
Other stakeholders

Question 2. Success factors
What factors do you think have contributed to the success of your work?
What conditions could have been taken into account in a better way?
List only one factor that you believe has been crucial to success in your work. Why?
What is the most important lesson you have learned and want to pass on to the next project?

Question 3. Overall assessment of project management effort
Project management has identified 10 success factors for DG3 in advance, including the following:

Apply best practices to achieve safe, interconnected, predictable and cost-effective implementation
What specific measures have been taken to apply best practices?
How challenging has it been to balance predictability and cost effectiveness in the project? Why has it been necessary to have c.120 people in Singapore to follow up the construction of the Topside?

Competent and sufficient internal and external resources
Has the project managed been successful? What specific measures have been taken?
How do you rate external resources (e.g. main contractor, package suppliers). Were they up to the challenge?
A lot of resources have been used to follow up package providers – why?

Motivated and coordinated team
Has the project succeeded with respect to this factor?
What specific measures have been taken?
What routines/processes have been used to uncover personality conflicts/poor chemistry among the team?

No-change
How difficult has it been to ensure the existence of this factor, given that there have been several challenges related to the engineering phase?

One team
Has the project been successful in achieving 'one team' as a success factor?
How challenging has it been to ensure 'one team'?
What specific measures have been taken to ensure 'one team' is a success factor?
Is there anything else you would like to add?

11.4 Appendix 4. Questionnaire – Suppliers

How did you experience the cooperation with Det norske?

Did you experience close follow-up from Det norske in the project? If so, how did you experience the close follow-up?

How did you experience the communication in the Ivar Aasen project?

Did you experience any challenges concerning the cooperation with your sub-contractors? If so, please describe one or several challenges that occurred during the project.

How did you experience the project in its entirety?

What do you consider are the main reasons for the success of the project?

What could have been done differently or better in the Ivar Aasen project organization?

Do you have any concrete advice or suggestions for improvements to the client's management team of Ivar Aasen?